CAR SICK

"Transport isn't working. *Car Sick* shows why, and sets out clearly what the answers are. A must-read for everyone interested in transport."—Stephen Joseph, Executive Director, Transport 2000

"Lynn Sloman is mainly known for her serious and careful studies of the impacts of transport policy initiatives. In this book she does something different, and new: she treats changes in travel behaviour from the point of view of the individual and family. Her characters are real, named people—her friends, and neighbours, and associates—who live like all of us in the pressures and constraints of everyday life in a car-dependent culture. She traces what actually happens when they have sought ways of leading a good life without a car, or while using a car sparingly. This is transport planning with a human scale, with a necessary, thought-provoking and encouraging message."—Phil Goodwin, Professor of Transport Policy, University of the West of England

CAR
SICK

Solutions for our Car-addicted Culture

Lynn Sloman

Chelsea Green Publishing Company
White River Junction, Vermont

First published in the UK in 2006
by Green Books Ltd,
Foxhole, Dartington,
Totnes, Devon TQ9 6EB

Published in the United States by
Chelsea Green Publishing Company
PO Box 428
White River Junction, VT 05001
802-295-6300
www.chelseagreen.com

Drawings and charts by Jennifer Johnson

ISBN 1-903998-76-X

Contents

Acknowledgements

The research for this book was funded by a fellowship in transport and the built environment from the Royal Commission for the Exhibition of 1851, and I am grateful to the Commissioners and the Secretaries to the Commission for their generous support and willingness to let me go where the research led. What I produced at the end was far different from what I had promised them at the beginning.

In particular, Alan Baxter gave me the encouragement to translate my rather dry research into what I hope is a more readable critique of the present transport system. I am also grateful to Peter Jones of the University of Westminster for the visiting fellowship which has facilitated a great deal of the research for this book. I have learnt a lot from Jillian Anable, Sally Cairns, Phil Goodwin, Alistair Kirkbride and Carey Newson, who were my co-researchers on a project funded by the Department for Transport to investigate how so-called 'soft' actions could reduce traffic. Some of the stories contained in this book are based on interviews originally carried out for that Department for Transport project, and I am grateful to those interviewees, named in the text, for the time and help they gave us. Similarly, I am grateful to the people I met while carrying out research on car traffic and schools (again, funded by the Department for Transport); those I spoke to in the course of a project on rural transport for Transport 2000, the Countryside Agency and Citizens Advice; and those I met while carrying out research on sustainable visitor travel for the National Trust. They are all named in the text, and it is their ideas and experience which have made it possible to write this book. I also thank Werner Brög, Denise Carlo, Nick Cavill, Adrian Davis, John Grimshaw, Christopher Heath, Stephen Joseph, Andy Rowland, Karen Rush and Teresa Walters for giving interviews or providing information. John Elford and Amanda Cuthbert at Green Books combined enthusiasm with patience, and I am grateful to them too.

Thank you to my family for all their encouragement. My father George Sloman helped with research, but moreover, has never once complained at my objections to cars even though the whole of his working life has in one way or another been associated with them. As a driving examiner, he taught me, as a then L-driver, that in taking charge of two tonnes of metal I bore a special and heavy responsibility to other non-armoured road users. In an era when many pedestrians and cyclists have been scared off the roads by careless driving, his perspective is more relevant than ever. And finally, thank you to my husband Ian Taylor whose ideas, questions and insights have helped to shape this book in very many ways, and without whom it would quite definitely never have been written.

Chapter 1

Cars 'R' Us

"The typical American male devotes more than 1,600 hours a year to his car. He sits in it while it goes and while it stands idling. He parks it and searches for it. He earns the money to put down on it and to meet the monthly installments. He works to pay for petrol, tolls, insurance, taxes and tickets. He spends four of his sixteen waking hours on the road or gathering his resources for it. And this figure does not take into account the time consumed by other activities dictated by transport: time spent in hospitals, traffic courts and garages; time spent watching automobile commercials or attending consumer education meetings to improve the quality of the next buy. The model American puts in 1,600 hours to get 7,500 miles: less than five miles per hour. In countries deprived of a transportation industry, people manage to do the same, walking wherever they want to go, and they allocate only three to eight per cent of their society's time budget to traffic instead of 28 per cent."

So wrote Ivan Illich in his book *Energy and Equity*, published in 1974.[1] Today, in Britain, the cost of running a car is lower, compared with typical annual salaries, than it was in America in the 1970s. But still, if you rerun Ivan Illich's calculation, the result is a startling one. The typical car-owning Briton today devotes nearly 1,300 hours a year to his or her car. It takes him over 500 hours to earn the money first to buy the car and then to pay for petrol, insurance, repairs and parking. He spends another 400 hours every year sitting in his car while it goes and while it waits in traffic jams. More than 250 hours are devoted to a myriad small tasks associated with a car: washing it, taking it to the garage for repair, filling it with petrol, looking for the car keys and walking to the car, de-icing the windscreen in winter, and finding a parking space at the end of every trip. Finally, he has to work about 100 hours every year to earn the money to pay the extra building society interest because he has chosen a house with a garage rather than one without.[2]

All in all, the typical British car driver in 2005 devoted three and a half of his sixteen waking hours to his car. For this time, he travels a little less than 10,000 miles per year. His average speed is less than 8 miles an hour— roughly the same as the speed at which he could travel on a bicycle.

Cars have come to dominate our culture and our daily lives. It is not simply a question of the amount of time we devote to driving them, earning the money to pay for them and attending to them. We are bombarded by images of cars from billboards, television screens and newspaper colour supplements. The imagery is preposterous: cars in the wilderness, parked on the rim of the Grand Canyon or driving across the sea like a hovercraft. Often the associations are with lifestyle choices and fashion: "It's so every season"; ". . . every season's must-have accessory"; "Think of all the stylish gadgets you can't leave the house without . . ."; ". . . You'll find that the inside is worthy of an interiors magazine." Advertising instils a sense that you are what you drive: that your car reveals to other people your status and outlook in life.

Cars permeate our society to such a degree that it is easy to forget what a recent phenomenon they are. Henry Ford may have started the production line rolling before the First World War, but it was not until the 1970s that the process of organising society around the car picked up pace. When the first stretch of the M1 motorway in Britain was being constructed in 1959, the 5,000 men who laboured to build it were brought to work in double-decker buses. Clearly, they were not part of the shiny new car-driving democracy that the road that they were building was intended for. Described by Transport Minister Ernest Marples as a "magnificent motorway opening up a new era in road travel", the M1 was at first only of any use to about one in four households, as three quarters of the population had no regular access to a car.

The opening of that first section of the M1 marked the start of a phenomenal and concentrated period of motorway construction, involving a scale of expenditure which seems inconceivable now. The pouring of concrete accelerated from the mid-1960s, and most of the motorway network was constructed in a brief period of just fifteen years. By the early 1980s, Britain's motorway network was substantially complete.

The new motorways, and other roads designed for travel at speed, paved the way for more change. Out-of-town supermarkets, located for easy access by car, began to appear during the 1970s. They were followed a decade later by non-food retail parks on the North American model, selling flat-pack furniture, DIY goods, electrical appliances and even children's toys. Then the massive regional shopping centres arrived, offering a whole-day shopping experience, including places to eat and children's play areas as well as hundreds of so-called 'high street' stores. The first multiplex cinema was opened in Milton Keynes in 1985, and followed by over a hundred more in out-of-town sites with acres of car parking close to motorway junctions.

In less than forty years, the car has become so intrinsic to the way we work, shop and spend our leisure time that it is almost inconceivable that we once managed without it. It is practically unimaginable that we might be able to use it less. To adapt the name of a famous store, itself a retail park product of the revolution in the way we travel, Cars 'R' Us.

The story of how we came to devote so much of our time, money and lives to the car is the story of a generation for whom car travel symbolised a new, high-tech, scientific age. They invested billions in the infrastructure to make it easy to travel fast by car. Civil engineers were the new gods, responsible for the design of grandiose schemes: Spaghetti Junction, hundreds of flyovers, thousands of concrete bridges. Houses were demolished and towns ripped apart to make space for cars to drive and be parked. In London, Bristol and elsewhere, fine Georgian squares were dug up, the plane trees uprooted, to make way for dual carriageways and underground car parks.

Pedestrian as an endangered species.

Old cuttings from local newspapers of the 1960s and 1970s show that there was often popular support for this bulldozing of towns and country-side, because people believed that it would solve the problems already being caused by traffic in their communities. In Kent, the county where I grew up, villagers from Swanley marched up the A20 to demand a bypass. I remember a street party in the village of Bridge to celebrate the opening of another bypass, for which the villagers had campaigned hard. There was bunting and cake, and a speech from the local MP. Everyone was jubilant. A bypass of Maidstone was celebrated for the same reason, that traffic would no longer plague the town centre. No one foresaw that the new roads would lead to huge increases in traffic. In May 1963, the first section of the M2 motorway was opened and the local newspapers reported that:

> The people of the Medway Towns can hardly believe their eyes. Traffic is flowing freely through Rochester and Chatham for the first time in many years. There are no long queues at the traffic lights in Strood and the volume of cars on the old Rochester bridge is remarkably light. All North Kent knows the reason; the first half of the M2 motorway has been opened and the Medway Towns will never be gridlocked by traffic again.[3]

The civil engineers and technocrats who were responsible for those grand schemes that were supposed to solve the traffic problem and ensure we would "never be gridlocked by traffic again" are still, today, an influential force. The reputation of their professions has survived surprisingly untarnished. Their message has been a little modified by events, but it is essentially the same. In the face of the fifteenfold increase in car traffic since 1950, and the incontrovertible damage that this has done, these powerful men have begun to whisper, at least some of the time, that we must do what we can to restrain the growth in car use. Not, you note, to reduce car use, but just to make it grow slightly more slowly. They no longer only argue for billions of pounds to be spent solely on motorways and flyovers. Now, they are arguing for billions to be spent on high-speed trains and trams as well. Some car journeys, they argue, could be replaced by public transport if we had faster trains for long-distance city-to-city trips, and radial tram networks shuttling between city centres and suburbs.

But then the same technocrats shake their heads. Unfortunately, they say, most car journeys are now too dispersed to multitudinous destinations for public transport to be an alternative. It is too late. There is nothing we can do about it. The only solution is more road construction, to ease congestion in the places where it is worst. In other words, more of the same, although with the bitter and expensive pill sweetened a little by the construction of some new trams and high-speed railways. Sometimes they suggest that road pricing, or congestion charging, could be used to combat the growth in traffic in city centres and on motorways, but they have no suggestion of what to do outside these hotspots—in the suburbs, small towns and countryside.

The technocrats have had forty years to show what they can do, and not only have they failed to civilise the car, they have made matters much worse. If you ask them now what their vision is, and where their new recommendations will lead us, they have little to say. But if you probe, it becomes clear that they say little because they know that the outcome of their recommended policies is an unpleasant and unsavoury one. Under their policy prescription, traffic will carry on getting worse. There will be more congestion—even if new roads are built at a rate far in excess of what can be afforded. There will be more concrete and tarmac. There will be more lifeless places where no one wants to be.

This is madness. The problem for the technocrats is that they have come to believe that increasing car use is an immutable fact of modern life. They fail to recognise that it is the policy choices made in the last 40 years that have created the world we live in today. They look at historic traffic trends—the result of the disastrous policies of the last 40 years—and extend those trends indefinitely into the future, and then they say, 'If traffic is going to rise, we will have to make room for it.' What they have done is to confuse cause and effect. They see traffic growth as a natural phenomenon, to which their bypasses and relief roads and multi-storey car parks were a response. They do not recognise that the bypasses and relief roads and multi-storey car parks, and the rash of car-scale development that they enabled, made driving more attractive and other means of travel more unpleasant.

* * *

This book is about an alternative approach. It is based on the evidence of some hundreds of quiet experiments, in Britain and elsewhere. These are not big-bang civil engineering schemes costing billions of pounds. They do not require massive construction sites (unlike new roads or railways), but they can be diffused across an entire city, improving the daily lives of millions of people. This approach involves cajoling people out of their cars for journeys where there is already a good alternative. It requires many thousands of small changes to the design of roads in and between towns to make them human-friendly again, instead of human-hostile. It also requires ambitious investment in simple forms of transport, especially buses and bicycles, which have the potential to meet at least 80 per cent of our daily travel needs. In gradual, and probably halting, steps, this approach leads to a reappraisal of the role of cars in our society, so that we think twice before hopping behind the steering wheel.

The focus of our effort should switch from a few grandiose engineering schemes to thousands of small initiatives. There is still a place for some of the light rail schemes advocated by today's technocrats, but it is a subsidiary place. This is because rather few of the 150 million or so journeys that are made in Britain every day lie along straight lines between suburbs and town centres that could be served by new tram networks. The technocrats were right when they pointed out that our journeys are much more complex than that. But their conclusion—that only the car could serve these other journeys—was fundamentally wrong.

Take London as an example. I recently sat in a meeting with the people who will decide the future transport strategy for the capital city. These people are talented and they care a great deal about making public transport in London better. But at heart they are engineers and they therefore tend to devote a disproportionate effort to new railways and tram lines.

One slide stood out amongst the hundreds that their teams presented to us, crammed with facts and figures. It showed the journey length profile for different types of travel: by car, bus, train, cycling and walking. Not surprisingly, most walking journeys are really quite short, and most train journeys are quite long. But if you look at journeys by car, bus and bicycle, they have an almost identical profile. Roughly half of all car trips in London are shorter than two miles, as are roughly half of all bus and cycle trips. Another third of car trips are between two and five miles long, and again, the same is true for bus and bike trips. In other words, most car journeys are very local, and of a similar length to the journeys that we make by bus or bicycle. And unlike tram lines, buses and bicycles can take you pretty well where you want.

Car dependence and its consequences are not simply technical problems, which can be solved by engineers with surveying poles and bulldozers. We

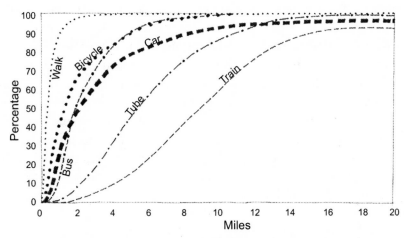

Figure 1: Trip lengths in London. The graph shows what percentage of trips is under a particular distance. Roughly half of bus, cycle and car trips are less than 2 miles.

need traffic engineers and civil engineers, but working at a smaller scale than that which some of them are accustomed to. Rather than using their skills on billion-pound projects to build wider faster roads, or on schemes to squeeze the largest possible number of cars through our city streets, we need them to work alongside urban designers to rehumanise the roads we already have. We need barefoot engineers, if you like, responding to the needs of local communities, using simple and inexpensive remedies to make it easier for people to get about on bike and bus and by foot. Many of these engineers are already employed by local councils. Some are very good at the job of rehumanising our streets; others would really rather that the human beings did not get in the way of their traffic-flow computer models.

But even the better engineers and urban designers need help to tackle the problem of car dependence. The problem is not just one of road design; it is also a problem of our own thoughtlessness. Driving has become the normal, habitual, expected means of transport, and other options are not even considered. Engineers cannot tackle this. The sort of people who might be able to tackle it—schooled in psychology and behavioural science, familiar with the techniques of marketing and advertising, skilled in the art of persuasion—are few and far between in local council transport departments, and are employed on short-term contracts with little back-up.

The evidence for the potential of this new approach, combining barefoot engineering with the softer skills of persuasion, is set out in the fol-

lowing pages. We will look at successful trial projects and city-wide initiatives in the UK, in the rest of Europe and across the world. The lessons are
not just for developed, car-dependent countries. They are also important
for countries where car ownership has not yet reached critical levels. In
China and India, the civil engineers and technical men from the World
Bank and the multinational consulting firms rule the roost. Billions of dol-
lars of development money are spent on elevated highways and express-
ways, and low-tech, sustainable, efficient means of transport are ignored
or despised. These countries are making the same mistakes that we made
in the 1970s, with even more far-reaching consequences for their societies
and for the global environment.

                                * * *

Ivan Illich showed that, far from saving time, the car consumes a quarter
of our waking lives. Instead of enabling us to do more, it constrains us to
doing less. Car-orientated transport policies have gobbled up time and
effort and money. The consequences of carrying on with the same old policies are grim. It is no good paying lip service to sustainable travel while
still devoting 90 per cent of the cash to more cars and more roads.

    Cars have come to control us, rather than the other way around, and
it is about time that we got back in charge again. There is no law that says
that traffic levels will always rise. As we will see later in this book, there
are towns where people now use their cars less than they did thirty years
ago. We can change our society so that it is not geared to cars, if we want
to. We can have less traffic within our communities, and less traffic shuttling to and fro between them. The future has not happened yet, and we
can decide what we want that future to look like.

Chapter 2

Cars: the ultimate mixed blessing

If you have one, a car has a lot of obvious advantages. It gets you to places that would be difficult to reach by public transport. It offers the luxury of not having to plan ahead—you can decide to nip into town, and there is no need to wait an hour for the next bus, or to time your trip so you can catch the last one home. If you can afford an expensive model, your car tells other people something about your status. For a seventeen-year-old, passing a driving test and getting wheels means you have entered the grown-up world.

Cars make us feel in control. There is no need to depend on neighbours or grown-up children, or on the bus turning up on time. We can use them to carry shopping or pick up flat-pack furniture. They function as a mobile shed when we are on holiday—though there are limits. A friend emailed us last summer about his plans to drop in with his partner and six-year-old daughter on their way back from holiday in Ireland: "After two weeks on holiday, we'll be heading back to London by car from Fishguard on the Saturday, so a detour and stopover for a night or two would fit really well," he said. "The complication is that we're not sure how much camping stuff we'll be able to fit in a car that will already be filled to the brim with toys, books, surfboards, kites, mountain boards, bikes—and that's just my stuff."

Then there is the security and privacy. If you are coming home late at night, a car gets you right to the front door. No need to walk from the bus stop through poorly lit residential streets, wondering whether the group of young men hanging around the street corner is about to mug you, or what is lurking in the shadows behind the bushes. If your teenage son is late to catch a train, you can pull a sweatshirt over your pyjamas and drive him to the station without any funny stares. (Imagine what would happen if you went for a walk in your pyjamas.) By contrast, travelling by bus involves sharing space with others. The buses in the rural area where I live are packed with schoolchildren first thing in the morning and mid-afternoon. They are noisy, they put their feet on the seats, they play-fight and they paint their nails and their friends' nails with varnish. As one 15-year-old commented in a local meeting about transport, "The school bus isn't ideal for adults to use. There isn't much room and our school bags are everywhere."

On a rainy day, a car means you can arrive at work in a smart suit, without wet trousers from the muddy water splashed up from wobbly paving slabs. Your socks will be dry and your shoes will still look smart. A habitual public transport user would have a coping strategy for rainy days, involving shoes that are waterproof and a good raincoat and umbrella. A driver may not have all the bad-weather wear, so a car feels all the more essential.

When you think of all the advantages of cars, it seems amazing that we managed perfectly well without them for centuries. But we did. In the last fifty years—less than one person's lifetime—car traffic has increased by 1,500 per cent. There were fewer than 2 million cars on the road in the UK in 1950, compared with nearly 25 million today. The shift to mass car ownership has brought with it some disadvantages that affect everybody, car users and non-car users alike. And that is the nub of the problem. Rather like passive smoking, indiscriminate car use affects you whether or not you drive a car. Like a smoker's cough, some of the adverse effects are obvious and felt immediately. Others—like a cancer—may not be apparent for decades. Worse, there is no way to opt out of the car-dependent society. If you are determined to avoid the effects of other people's cigarettes, you can do so, by choosing carefully which pubs and restaurants you visit. But in a society organised around cars, the effects of the infernal combustion engine are felt everywhere.

People have lots of different reasons for disliking car culture, and they are often not the obvious ones that are quoted by transport ministers and journalists, such as congestion and pollution. My personal list of objections runs like this.

Objection 1: Fast cars hog the best routes
At speeds above about 30 miles an hour, cars are intimidating. They hog the best routes from place to place. If you walk or cycle along a country

lane, you must always be looking over your shoulder for a car bearing down on you at 60 miles an hour. On main roads in rural areas, where there is often no pavement, you end up walking through the long wet grass and mud on the verge. Some cyclists say they do not mind cycling on high-speed rural main roads, but, like many others, I always have to steel myself to cycle the 6 miles from my village into the local market town, and I know many people who say they would like to cycle but do not do so because it is too scary.

In the area where I live, the Dyfi Valley, the council and local community groups got together to ask residents what they thought needed to be done about traffic and transport in the area. More than a thousand people from nearly 500 households responded. The single issue that was mentioned more than any other was that people wanted to be able to walk or cycle along the main roads. People said things like:

> At the moment we are afraid to walk to town because of speeding traffic. Since I have lived in Penegoes, in the summer months you are housebound because you are afraid to walk along the road (so come on let's get a footpath)!!!

> I would cycle, but I'm frightened off the main road, especially where there's a bend.

> It's not safe to walk on the main road—so you sit in the car. Walking you can be squashed in the hedge.

> I've observed speeds of 50 + [miles an hour] and I've had to dive into the hedge myself.

> I walk with my daughter down to school [along the main road] and the drivers don't slow down at all.

> The speed limit of 40 miles an hour—it's taken twenty years to get that. But then it's the enforcement of it. You can come along this road [past the school]—it has a 30 mile an hour limit, but people drive at 50 miles an hour.

One thing leads to another. As one of the residents commented, because it is not safe to walk, people end up driving, themselves adding to the number of cars on the main road, and in turn deterring another person from walking or cycling. This sort of self-reinforcing positive feedback crops up time and again, as we shall see.

Objection 2: Death of local variety and our choice of where to shop

Mass car ownership has favoured big retailers at the expense of small independent shopkeepers. Large supermarkets and out-of-town shopping cities are only viable if millions of customers can reach them, travelling long distances and transporting their own goods away afterwards. As car ownership has increased, the superstores have taken advantage of the greater mobility of their customers by building larger stores which have a wider range of goods and can therefore attract people from a larger catchment. The large scale of their operation means they can cut prices, so smaller shops cannot compete.

The supermarkets are eager to give the impression that they are offering shoppers more choice than ever before, but the harsh truth is that we now have much less choice of where to shop than our parents' generation. Between 1961 and 1997, the total number of grocery retailers fell by 80 per cent, from 147,000 to less than 29,000.[1] Independent fresh food outlets, such as bakers, butchers, fishmongers and greengrocers, had a 40 per cent drop in sales between 1995 and 2000. Even the local newsagent is in decline, with a 9 per cent drop in shops selling confectionery, tobacco and newspapers in just three years between 1997 and 2000.[2] The total number of superstores in Britain is now a little over 1,000, and these 1,000 outlets now capture more than half of the money we spend on groceries.[3]

Mass car ownership is not the only reason for this contraction in choice of where to shop. But it is an important contributory factor. The most significant study of the stranglehold large supermarkets now have on the retail sector was commissioned by the Department of the Environment from property experts Hillier Parker in 1998. Their surveys showed that if a car is available, it is almost certain to be used for food shopping. Instead of considering whether to shop in the town centre or at the out-of-town superstore, and then deciding whether to take the bus or drive, we take the decision the other way around. We decide what means of transport we will use and then choose the shopping location that is most convenient. Not surprisingly, shoppers who have decided to travel by car prefer to patronise the out-of-town store with its large, free car park. The supermarkets are fond of saying that all they are doing is providing the service that people want, and in a sense this is true. As car ownership has gone up, we have chosen to drive to the shops, and once we made this decision we needed the tarmacked acres on offer at the out-of-town or edge-of-town superstore.

The change from a nation of small shopkeepers to a nation whose grocery shopping is dominated by just four major international players—Asda/Walmart, Tesco, Sainsbury's and Safeway/Morrisons—has taken place over the same period as the explosion of car ownership. I vividly and slightly uncannily remember a prescient item on the local television news when I was a child in the late 1960s, about the opening of the first of a new chain of self-service supermarkets. "Customers will be able to serve themselves rather than wait for a shop assistant," the reporter explained, "but there are worries about the effect of the new supermarkets on existing shops."

The change may have been spread over forty or fifty years, but every time you decide to drive to one of the out-of-town giants, you are contributing to the death of a small high-street shop. The Hillier Parker study found that the opening of a new out-of-town or edge-of-centre superstore can have a dramatic impact on local retailers. In Fakenham, a small market town in Norfolk, the proportion of local people shopping in the town centre fell by 64 per cent when a new out-of-town Safeway opened in 1994. One of the two small town-centre supermarkets closed, and turnover at other town-centre shops fell by up to a quarter. In St Neots, turnover at one town-centre store fell by nearly 30 per cent when an out-of-town Tesco opened in 1995, despite the store extending its opening hours. In Leominster, nine town-centre food shops closed when an out-of-town Safeways opened in 1992. This meant there were about a third fewer food shops in Leominster town centre. The number of vacant shops more than doubled. The surviving independent food shops experienced a general decline in business, with turnover at one shop falling by 30 per cent.

With the loss of thousands of small shops, we have lost variety and local distinctiveness; it no longer matters whether you are shopping in Aberdeen or Eastbourne, as the products on offer are the same. This is not just nostalgia for a vanished way of life. Small independent shops can source local products, so more of the money you spend in them stays in the local economy. A proportion of the profits will be recycled into other local businesses.

Take the Quarry Shop, an independently owned wholefood shop in Machynlleth, my local market town. It stocks bread from a small bakery in Talerddig, eggs from a farm near Newtown, cream and yogurt from a dairy company near Aberystwyth, milk from Pembrokeshire, jams and chutneys from Tywyn, pasta sauces from Newtown again, honey from Machynlleth itself, cheese from a company in Snowdonia, butter from

Pembrokeshire, cakes from Aberaeron, mayonnaise from Ystradgynlais, Red Kite drinks from near Cardigan, flour from a family mill near Newtown, jams, peanut butter and tahini spreads packed in Corwen, and ice creams and meringues from Mary's Farmhouse, based in Crymych.

By contrast, large superstores only work because they are backed up by national and international supply chains. Standing at a superstore checkout, few of the products in your shopping basket will be from local suppliers, and almost all the money you spend will be sucked straight out of your local area, repatriated to shareholders who may not even be based in the same country.

Objection 3: Loss of local services

Small shops are not the only local services that have been closing. The transformation of the retail industry has been mirrored by steady closure of local post offices, banks, small hospitals, job centres and magistrates' courts. The planners think that they will be able to reduce costs by having fewer buildings to run. The people who pay the price are the most vulnerable in society—the sick, the unemployed, the poor and those seeking access to justice. Among the poorest households (those whose income is in the lowest 20 per cent), less than half own a car. Most pensioner households (69 per cent) do not own a car. Most single-parent families (56 per cent) are also without a car. For these people, bank, post office, magistrates' court and job centre closures, or the move of a town-centre hospital to an out-of-town site, cause great inconvenience and in some cases hardship.

The records kept by Citizens Advice Bureaux provide a litany of tales of the problems people suffer because services are being centralised and local offices closed. I met Sue Edwards, a social policy officer for Citizens Advice, when we worked together on a project looking at transport in the countryside. As part of the project, she asked local CABs to tell her about the transport difficulties their clients faced. We received many pages of case-note summaries. "Our bureaux deal with transport problems on a daily basis," Sue told me. She showed me a few examples. A single mother on income support had been in touch with a CAB in Shropshire to ask for help when she was summoned to attend court for a review of her financial circumstances. The court was over 40 miles away, and she simply did not know how she would be able to get there. The trip would have involved two buses, or a taxi which would have cost £44, a third of her weekly income. In Derbyshire, a CAB was contacted by a man who lived in a remote rural area and had just lost his job. The closure of the local job centre meant he had to make a 36-mile round trip by infrequent public transport to another town, to sign on and look for vacancies. Sue told me that in some rural areas, people get into debt because they cannot afford a car, but cannot manage without one. A 62-year-old man in Lincolnshire got in touch with his local CAB because he lived in a village which had very few amenities and poor public transport, and he felt he had to run a car. He had run up an overdraft and had to take out loans to cover bills for the car.[4]

In the village of Liss, Hampshire, all three bank branches—Lloyds, Barclays and NatWest—closed in quick succession in the mid-1990s. Writing in the summer of 2000, local resident Margaret Effenberg described the problem: "We are now forced to travel to Petersfield or Liphook to visit the bank or withdraw money—a round journey of 10 miles each visit."[5] Liss is a sizeable village, with a population of 6,500. Margaret calculated that overall, Liss villagers had to travel a staggering 1 million extra miles a year to use their bank. Most of the villagers made the new trip by car, which was inconvenient and added to traffic but did not entail real difficulty. But for some the round trip was a problem. "The extra travel is particularly affecting older and disabled people," Margaret explained. "37 per cent of the villagers are aged over 60 and 20 per cent have a disability that limits mobility." Local people were also concerned about the knock-on effects of the bank closures on local shops. The local retailers were faced with making a round trip to Petersfield each day to bank the day's takings, and the loss of the banks affected residents' shopping habits. As Margaret commented, "If you go to the bank in Petersfield, you're not going to come back to shop in Liss, are you?"

Margaret and others campaigned hard against the bank closures; as a result of their work there are now several cash machines in Liss, and the post office offers some limited banking facilities. But the banks have not reopened, and damage has been done. "It's now very difficult for small businesses in Liss," Margaret explained. "Some businesses have closed and several premises are now vacant. Six months ago an organic vegetable shop opened, but they are now closing. People are shopping out of the area." High car ownership led to closure of the banks, and now those two factors working together are undermining a once-thriving local economy.

In Norwich, the city hospital moved out of the town centre to a site just off the city's southern bypass. The move was resisted by local people, who argued that it would be more difficult for out-patients and visitors to reach the new hospital, and it would cause an increase in traffic, which in turn would mean more dangerous roads, worse air pollution and fewer people able to get healthy exercise by walking or cycling. In other words, more ill people—hardly what the NHS wants. Denise Carlo was involved in a campaign to try to stop the hospital move. After the new hospital opened, all her fears about access difficulties came true. She told me: "Since the hospital opened, the transport situation has worsened. Even more car parking has been provided and the bus services have been dreadful." Out-patients and visitors now have little choice but to drive.

When fewer people had a car, services like health care, banks, courts and unemployment offices were provided in places that people could reach by bicycle or bus. Today, the Government and private companies get away with closing down these local, easily accessed services, because most people can reach the more distant locations by car. If you own a car, it is a minor inconvenience when the local post office closes, or the old city hospital moves. But for the old, the poor and the sick it is now more difficult. These closures are only explicable if you assume that everyone has access to a car, or that everyone who matters has access to a car. The planners can get away with it because we are such a heavily motorised society.

Objection 4: Loss of social glue

There are only 24 hours in the day, and only 365 days in the year. No matter how hard we try to squeeze more activities into our waking hours, we come up against this limiting factor. High-speed travel has enabled us to come into contact with many more people, over a far wider area. But the down side of this is that we spend less time in any one place. As John Adams puts it in an essay on the phenomenon of hypermobility, "If people in their travelling choose to spread themselves more widely, they must spread themselves more thinly."[6] This might not matter, were it not for the fact that we are all spreading ourselves more thinly. The chances of walking down the high street and accidentally bumping into someone you know are lower. Without all those opportunities for informal, unplanned contact, the street is a less friendly place, filled not with neighbours, friends and acquaintances but with strangers.

Some places can withstand this phenomenon better than others. On islands, or in small market towns with a large rural hinterland, geography prevents all the criss-crossing trips between multiple workplaces, shopping centres, multiplex entertainment venues and suburbs that characterise less isolated areas. There are fewer possible destinations, so there is more likelihood of a chance meeting with someone you know. Here in Machynlleth, there are some thirty small shops catering for a population of about 2,000 people in the town and another 10,000 who live in the surrounding hamlets and farms. The nearest big supermarket is 18 miles away in Aberystwyth, too far for most people to bother to drive on roads that are thankfully still winding and not important enough to be straightened, broadened or otherwise 'upgraded'. That means that people's shopping and social activity are mostly focused in the same place: roughly two-thirds of households shop in Machynlleth, and for roughly half it is the main place for an evening out. The result is that you cannot go shopping or out to watch a film without coming across people you know. A walk down the main street to buy a pint of milk is punctuated by greetings, smiles and short conversations. On market day, these might be with Eleri, who sells home-made cakes; Ruth and Nick at one of the vegetable stalls; the fishmonger, who always smiles even though I don't know him; the butcher, who always waves even though we are vegetarian and do not buy his reputedly excellent meat; Amanda and Predr in the wholefood shop; Barbara who runs the telecentre; Annie at the café below the flat we used to rent; Jonathan and Yonnie who have opened a new bike shop; Cyril, who teaches Welsh, and his wife, Alison; Liza, who used to be in my Welsh class and is the cousin of the husband of my friend in Norwich; Nat who publishes the local events diary; Teresa, who works for a local community group . . . and so on.

That sort of chance contact is much less likely where there are many choices of possible destination, each serving a large and overlapping catchment. It is not that people in small towns are friendlier than people who live in big cities or suburbs. Rather, if you live in a suburb of, say, Leeds, work 20 miles away in York, shop at any one of several large stores within five miles of home and have a childminder who lives three miles in the opposite direction, the opportunity for 'just bumping into so-and-so' is much less. High mobility and the choice of many destinations comes at the price of less incidental, unplanned social contact.

Professor Robert D. Putnam has carried out some fascinating research on the breakdown of social ties amongst Americans. Based on masses of data going back to the 1930s and earlier, he concluded that Americans are less involved in their local communities now than ever before, and that this loss of 'social capital' has happened across social classes and the generations. Greater mobility is one of the factors to blame.

> In round numbers the evidence suggests that each additional ten minutes in daily commuting time cuts involvement in community affairs by 10 per cent—fewer public meetings attended, fewer committees chaired, fewer petitions signed, fewer church services attended, less volunteering, and so on. In fact, although commuting time is not quite as powerful an influence on civic involvement as education, it is more important than almost any other demographic factor. And time diary studies suggest that there is a similarly strong negative effect of commuting time on informal social interaction. Strikingly, increased commuting time among the residents of a community lowers average levels of civic involvement even among non-commuters.[7]

People in highly mobile societies travel further and come into shallow fleeting contact with many thousands of their fellow citizens, but the downside is that they have much less opportunity for repeated informal contact with a smaller circle of acquaintances in their immediate neighbourhood. Someone who walks out of the front door and climbs straight into a car parked on the driveway simply never gets to know the neighbours living five or six doors down the street. They might as well be strangers. A world filled with strangers feels a lot less safe than one peopled by familiar faces, and that, maybe, goes part of the way to explaining why we now feel we live in a less trusting society than fifty years ago.

Objection 5: Owning a car makes you fat

Most people now lead inactive lifestyles. The amount of time we spend doing something physically active, like walking the dog, DIY around the house, or playing sport, is not enough to burn off the calories from the food we eat. In the past, more people had jobs that required physical effort, but now only a minority are engaged in manual work. The advent of 'labour-saving' devices like washing machines and vacuum cleaners has reduced the amount of effort needed for everyday household tasks, and we spend more leisure time than any previous generation in low-energy mode, watching television or using computers. Finally, mass car ownership has led most people to drive for short trips that previous generations would have walked or cycled. The result is that there is now an epidemic of obesity. To call it an epidemic is no exaggeration: nearly a quarter of all British adults are clinically obese, and amongst middle-aged people the proportion is even greater. Many more are overweight, even if they are not clinically obese. Average weights and average waistlines are bigger now than they have ever been. It is normal to be fat.

Sedentary habits not only make us fat but also have wider effects on health. People who are physically inactive are more likely to die early. They face almost twice the risk of dying from coronary heart disease than more active people, and they have a greater risk of contracting cancer and diabetes. Physical inactivity is as significant a cause of chronic disease as smoking cigarettes, according to the Government's Chief Medical Officer.[8]

Obesity is good news for the dieting industry. According to market research by Mintel, about a quarter of adults in the UK are trying to lose weight most of the time, or in other words are on a semi-permanent diet.[9] Manufacture of reduced-fat or low-calorie foods is booming. But dieting without exercise is a largely futile activity. Another report by Mintel found that people who thought of themselves as very overweight were more likely than average to be trying to keep their fat intake down and to eat five portions of fresh fruit and vegetables per day, and rarely ate sweets. While the link between weight and diet was weak, there was a much clearer link between weight and exercise habits. About 30 per cent of those who did little or no exercise said they thought of themselves as 'quite a bit overweight'. In contrast, only 10 per cent of regular exercisers said this.[10]

Why are we facing this crisis of obesity? It is clear that there is an imbalance between the calories we are consuming and the energy we are expending, but how much of the blame should be pinned on less active lifestyles? Perhaps, after all, growing waistlines might be the result of us eating more food, or more fatty food, than twenty years ago?

Andrew Jebb and Susan Prentice considered this in a paper for the *British Medical Journal* titled 'Obesity in Britain: gluttony or sloth?'[11] They pointed out that while our waistlines have expanded, average calorie intake has actually gone down. Between 1970 and 1990, the incidence of obesity trebled, yet the calories consumed at home, in meals out, and in alcohol, soft drinks and confectionery fell by a fifth. As they say: "The paradox of increasing obesity in the face of decreasing food intake can only be explained if levels of energy expenditure have declined faster than energy intake, thus leading to an over-consumption of energy relative to a greatly reduced requirement." In other words, the cause of the nation's growing waistlines is societal sloth.

Nick Cavill is an expert in physical activity and health. He pointed out to me the seriousness of the obesity epidemic. "There's a generation of children being born now who could be the first generation to have a lower life expectancy than their parents. Life expectancy has risen because we've eradicated many common diseases. Now what we are seeing is that people are dying of the non-communicable diseases, like coronary heart disease and diabetes, and these are linked to obesity." Our bodies were honed by millions of years of evolution to be physically active, and our genes cannot keep up with the radical change in lifestyle of the last fifty years. As Nick explained, "Our caveman ancestors chased bison—that's what their bodies were adapted to do. As a species, we were incredibly active thousands of years ago, quite active hundreds of years ago, and now, in the space of less than a generation, we have become almost completely inactive. Nature intended us to move around, and we're going against that."

This is not to say that we all have to start chasing bison. Quite small amounts of physical activity can increase fitness, reduce the risk of chronic illness and reduce weight. The official international advice is that 30 minutes of moderate exercise five days a week is enough to deliver substantial health benefits, although more than that—about 45 minutes a day—may be needed to lose weight. The even better news is that the exercise does not all have to be taken at one go. As Nick Cavill told me, "You can do it in bite-sized chunks. The fitness benefit from three ten-minute walks, five days a week, is almost identical to that from walking continuously for thirty minutes on five days." There is even evidence to suggest that people who take their exercise in shorter chunks lose more weight than those who do it all at one go. The crucial thing, though, is that the exercise must be regular, almost every day. Since few people have the time or motivation to go to the gym or swimming pool five days a week, this in practice means putting physical activity back into our everyday lives. We need to get incidental exercise when doing something else, rather than find extra time which can be dedicated to purposeless exercise on a treadmill or exercise bike.

And this is where the spotlight turns back to cars. Figures collected by the Government's national travel survey show that over the course of a year, the typical Briton does 370 short trips (that is, trips of between 0 and 5 miles) by car. That is equivalent to one short car trip per day. Walking the shortest trips and cycling the slightly longer ones would give almost exactly thirty minutes of moderate exercise per day. For many of these short trips, walking or cycling is as quick, or even quicker, than driving and finding a parking space, so no time penalty would be incurred. Purposeful 'active travel'—that is, walking or cycling on a short trip that had to be made anyway—could on its own be enough to save tens of thousands of premature deaths every year.

Nick Cavill reviewed dozens of medical research studies confirming that cars have made us fat, and using them less could make us thin again. First, he pointed out that there is circumstantial evidence of the link between body weight and active travel. "If you look at the countries in Europe that have low levels of obesity, they tend to be the ones where more people cycle, and vice versa." The correlation is not clear-cut, but it seems to be there. Denmark and the Netherlands have the lowest levels of obesity in the European Union, and the highest levels of cycling. Britain, on the other had, has just about the highest level of obesity in Europe, and very low levels of cycling.

There are lots of studies which show the health benefits of active travel, which Nick pointed out to me.[12] The Honolulu Heart Programme found that the mortality rate in men who walked less than one mile a day was nearly twice that of men who walked more than two miles a day. A study of 9,000 Whitehall civil servants found that those who cycled regularly— for example at least an hour a week as part of a round trip to work—had less than half the incidence of coronary heart disease than those who took no physical activity during the course of the nine-year study.

The Copenhagen Heart Study looked at the health of more than 30,000 people. People who regularly cycled to work, cycling an average 30 minutes per day, had a 40 per cent lower risk of dying during the period of the study than people who did not cycle regularly. This was the case even after the researchers had made allowance for other factors, including the amount of leisure-time exercise.

But the study that clinches it is from China. Colin Bell, Keyou Ge and Barry Popkin collected data on obesity and car ownership for over 4,700 Chinese adults.[13] They also followed about half of the project participants over a period of eight years, to find out how their weight changed. Car ownership in China is growing, but it is still fairly low, so it is the ideal place to find out what happens to obesity levels when people acquire a car for the first time. By contrast, car ownership in Britain is already so high that it would be difficult to do the same study.

Among the 4,700 adults in the study, the odds of being obese were 70 per cent greater for men if they owned a car. For women, the odds were

85 per cent greater: car ownership very nearly doubled the risk of being obese. In calculating these odds, Colin Bell and his colleagues made allowance for a wide range of factors. For example, it might be that rich people tended to eat more and have less physically demanding jobs as well as being able to afford a car. The calculation of the odds of being obese was therefore adjusted for these other factors, taking account of age, work and leisure activity, energy intake, smoking status, alcohol consumption, income, education, household ownership of a computer and television, and urban residence. With all these other factors being equal, men and women who owned a car were much more likely to be overweight.

Among the people Bell and his colleagues followed for eight years, some 13 per cent acquired a vehicle during that period. Bell found that "motorised vehicle acquisition was an important predictor of weight gain in men". Interestingly, the same effect was not seen with women, perhaps because it tended to be the men in any household who had first call on the car once it was purchased. Compared with those who did not acquire a vehicle, men who bought a car gained an extra 2 kilograms in weight.

The conclusion from the Chinese study is inescapable. If you buy a car, you will put on weight. You will be twice as likely to become clinically obese, and this will lead inexorably to poorer health.

Objection 6: Cars are killing machines

Today, and tomorrow, and the day after that, ten families in Britain will have their world turned upside down for ever, with the death of a child, parent, brother or sister in a car crash. Over 3,000 people are killed every year in Britain. Over 30,000 are seriously injured, in some cases losing their sight or their legs, or suffering permanent brain damage, so that their own lives and the lives of the people who care for them will never be the same again. There are also uncounted numbers of people who suffer from grief and depression for decades after the death of a loved one, sometimes themselves committing suicide years later.

The charity RoadPeace supports victims of road crashes and their families. It was founded by Brigitte Chaudhry, whose own son was killed in a car crash. Five years ago, I worked with Brigitte to try to persuade the Government to toughen up the law on speeding, because it was clear that a great many avoidable deaths happened because vehicles were being driven much too fast. Through working with Brigitte, I met some of the members of RoadPeace who had suffered the loss of a close family member. Many of them wrote personal letters to Prime Minister Tony Blair to press for lower speed limits and stricter speed enforcement. These are two of their stories.

Joanne Love's son, Thomas, was sixteen and a half when he was killed. He was on the pavement just outside the park in London where he had played all his life. The speed limit on the road was 30mph, but the driver of the car was travelling much faster. Joanne Love said in her letter:

> This is the first time I have ever written to you on an issue but this one is very dear to my heart as my son Thomas Love was killed by someone driving a stolen car at well over the 30mph speed limit. Thomas was killed on 14 May 1999 on Green Lanes, right next to Clissold Park. . . . To add to the horror my younger son Josh was with his brother when he was hit by the car. I cannot imagine what my son and their friends went through in those terrible moments. I could write for pages about the effect the unlawful killing of my beautiful child has had upon myself and my family. Our lives have been completely destroyed by the actions of another person driving at speed. Speeding cars kill people every single day and we as a nation just don't seem to care very much about that at all. Of course it is always something that you hear about, not something that happens to you. Well, it happened to my son. He is dead and his brother Josh and I somehow have to exist in this world without him.

Roger and Joanne Browning suffered the death of their five-month-old daughter in a car crash on a rural road in Surrey. They were driving on a winding country lane, with their daughter strapped in a car seat. They wrote:

> The road we were travelling on [had] a 60mph limit, clearly a lethal speed but, nevertheless, the blanket 'national' limit under which most rural roads fall. Because of the nature of the road, we were travelling at about 35mph, which we considered safe. The car that collided head-on with our vehicle on a bend was judged by police to be travelling at 60mph. Although our daughter was killed in the crash, the driver was only fined £250 because, as her lawyer pointed out, the driver had been travelling within the speed limit and so her standard of driving could be judged as merely careless. Almost six years after the crash our lives are still seriously blighted. Our daughter, who in her five months showed herself to be a happy and healthy child, has been robbed of life; one of the worst aspects of her death was how needless and preventable it was.

Health-and-safety-at-work experts talk about the 'accident pyramid'. At the tip of the pyramid is someone's death or a serious injury. But below

that there may be ten people who are slightly injured, and below that, perhaps a few tens of incidents where property is damaged but nobody is
hurt, and below that again, perhaps several hundred near-miss incidents
which could all too easily have led to a death, that are thought of as 'a
lucky escape'. To stop people being killed, it is no good relying on luck.
You have to change the unsafe working practices and bad habits at the
base of the pyramid. These bad habits seem, on the face of it, trivial.
Ninety-nine times out of a hundred they do not result in anyone being
hurt, and so workers and managers may assume that they do not matter.
In fact, 'accidents' are never accidental—they are the predictable one-time-
in-a-hundred consequences of repeated potentially dangerous acts. The
only way to reduce the number of accidents is to systematically change the
risky behaviour that gives rise to them.

The same approach should be applied to the roads, but it is not. Nearly
ten people are killed in car crashes in Britain every day. Another 250 are seriously injured, and about 1,000 people are slightly hurt. Beneath these head-
line statistics there could be as many as 20,000 crashes where a vehicle is
damaged but nobody is hurt. And beneath this again, there is an unknown,
but very large, number of potentially dangerous practices and bad habits.[14]
Ninety-nine times out of a hundred, these do not result in a crash. People
overtake on a blind bend and there is nothing coming the other way. They
drive at 40 miles an hour in a 20 mile an hour zone outside a children's playground and no child steps off the road unexpectedly. But one time in a hun-

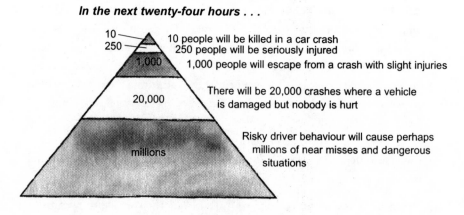

Figure 2: The accident pyramid.

dred there is a car driving the other way, or a child crossing the road.

If we treated road safety as seriously as we treat health and safety at work, we would systematically make it impossible for drivers to behave in this risky way. We would use legislation, road design and law enforcement to ensure that drivers drove within their own capabilities and those of their vehicles, and made allowance for unpredicted actions by others.

The most widespread risky behaviour is driving too fast. By this I do not only mean breaking the speed limit, although this is commonplace. As Roger and Joanne Browning found, the speed limit is sometimes far in excess of a safe speed. To eliminate the unsafe behaviour at the base of the accident pyramid, we would cut the speed limit to 20mph wherever people lived, played, shopped or went to school. The limit on narrow country lanes would be much lower than the current 60mph. Speed limiters in every vehicle would ensure everyone kept to the safe limits. Speed cameras would be widely used to enforce the law and drivers who persistently overrode their car's speed limiter and broke the limit would be banned from driving for life. If we did these things, thousands of people, including Joanne Love's son and Roger and Joanne Browning's baby daughter, could still be alive today.

"Ah, but it just isn't reasonable to expect everyone to drive so slowly," people say. I do not really think there is any answer to this, except to ask, is it reasonable to tell a mother or father that their child has been killed for the sake of a few saved minutes?

As it is, many schools and villages are on roads where speed limits are 40mph, 50mph or even 60mph, and peak speeds on these roads tend to be even higher than the legal limits. Parents keep children indoors because it is not safe to go out, and that in itself is a tragedy because it means that children are never allowed to do their own thing, away from adult supervision, as all previous generations did. Instead of biking round to a friend's house, or walking half a mile to the park to collect conkers, they have to wait for an adult to be free to take them.

Speed cameras are effective at reducing speeds and saving lives, on average reducing deaths and serious injuries by more than a third. However, the Government sets guidelines which say that they may only be used where at least four people have already been killed or seriously injured. One, two or three deaths are not enough. Thousands of communities want a camera but have been told that they cannot have one because not enough people have been killed.[15]

Our society is paralysed with fear from taking effective action against this annual slaughter. Lower speed limits and wider use of speed cameras are labelled 'anti-motorist' by those who enjoy driving fast, who believe that their quick reactions, judgement and superior skill give them the right to decide their own speed. These speed merchants are, by the way, mostly male: men commit 97 per cent of dangerous driving offences, 94 per cent of offences causing death and serious injury, 85 per cent of careless driving offences and 83 per cent of speeding offences.[16] The right to drive a car at a speed of your own choosing has become more important than the right of 3,000 people per year to stay alive.

My father taught me to drive when I was 17. He impressed on me that as a driver you are in control of a dangerous machine. The unexpected will happen—a child will run into the road, a cyclist will wobble, or a driver will pull out of a side road without seeing you. In all these circumstances, you are the person in control of a potentially lethal weapon, and as such, you carry a special and heavy responsibility. In our society's growing addiction to the car, we seem to have lost sight of that point.

Objection 7: Gas-guzzling is killing the planet

Every car journey adds to the carbon dioxide in the atmosphere. In Britain, road transport uses 42 million tonnes of oil per year, in the form of petrol or diesel. This is more than all the energy used by British industry, and over a quarter of total energy use for all purposes—industry, business, travel, domestic heating and power.[17] The petrol and diesel break down into carbon dioxide, water and a variety of poisonous gases.

For over 10,000 years, the amount of carbon dioxide in the atmosphere was constant at about 270 parts per million by volume. However, with the start of the industrial revolution, we began burning large quantities first of coal, then of oil and gas, releasing carbon that had been buried deep in the Earth for millennia. As a result of this, carbon dioxide concentrations in the atmosphere began rising, and have now reached 370 parts per million by volume. This is the highest level of carbon dioxide in the atmosphere since the Pliocene period, three million years ago.[18] High concentrations of carbon dioxide act like the glass of a greenhouse, letting the sun's energy through to the Earth, but stopping the heat getting out again. As a result, our planet is getting warmer, and that is causing irreversible changes to the climate and possibly disastrous effects for all life on Earth.

The rapidity of change in the amount of carbon dioxide in the Earth's atmosphere is without geological precedent, and it is this speed of change, which leaves little time for natural systems to adapt, that makes climate change so serious. We are likely to see severe effects of climate change within the lifetimes of people in their thirties today. They include:

- Mass extinction of species. As glaciers melt and sea levels rise, many coastal habitats of major migratory bird populations will disappear, and the birds will disappear with them. Much of the Arctic icecap will melt, eliminating the habitat of seals, walruses and polar bears. A wide variety of habitats and ecosystems will be threatened, including coral reefs and atolls, mangrove swamps, boreal and tropical forests and alpine meadows. One study published in the scientific journal *Nature* suggested that without drastic action to tackle climate change, between a sixth and a third of all animal and plant species on the land could inevitably be destined for extinction by 2050, either because they have no climatically suitable habitat left, or because they are unable to migrate to new habitats fast enough to keep up with the changing climate.[19]

- Coastal flooding and erosion. Sea level rise and storm surges will cause severe social and economic effects for communities living in low-lying coastal areas or on small islands. Worldwide, tens of millions of people may be made homeless, and there will be large-scale movements of refugees away from flooded areas. The Royal Commission on Environmental Pollution concluded that "nations and communities will face changes in the environment that will force them to make drastic alterations in their ways of life and in land use and other practices. In some parts of the world millions of people might become environmental refugees, with widespread suffering, economic disruption, and consequent social and political instability."[20] In Britain, major estuaries and the whole of the east coast, from Hull down to the Isle of Wight, will be threatened with shoreline erosion. Coastal defences will be destroyed, and villages and ancient landscapes will have to be given up to the sea.[21]

- Extreme weather events. There will be many more extreme weather events, such as heat waves and disastrous storms causing floods, landslides, avalanches and mudslides. Freak events that would have been expected to happen once every hundred years could happen every three years. In England and Wales, over 4 million people live on floodplains along rivers, estuaries and coasts which are at risk of flooding during severe storms. These people will face extensive damage or destruction of their homes, the threat of repeat flooding, and on top of all that, possible withdrawal of insurance cover, effectively making their homes unsaleable.[22]

- Health Risks. Climate change will increase threats to human health. There will be more heat-related deaths. Many more people will be at risk of diseases like malaria and dengue fever. Infectious diseases generally will rise, and diseases which are currently unknown outside the tropics will spread north to Europe. Some areas will suffer from droughts or severe water shortage, leading to use of contaminated water supplies.[23]

These effects are not a worst-case scenario. They are based on the climate responding in a linear way to increasing levels of atmospheric carbon dioxide. However, there is also the risk of runaway climate change occurring. Until very recently, models for climate change have had two major defects. The first is that, rather remarkably, they have not included the response of biological systems. The second is that they have assumed that the planet's responses to climate change will not show any step changes; that is, that we will not cross any thresholds at which some of the Earth's systems start to behave fundamentally differently from the way they behave now.

Recent models have started to look at these things and the results are alarming. For example, they show that around 2050, the Amazon basin is likely to change from being a massive absorber of carbon dioxide to being an emitter. With the rise in global temperatures, the Amazon will get drier, which will lead to more forest fires and forest die-back, and eventually to the collapse of the entire Amazon rainforest and its replacement by savannah or semi-desert. As the rainforest dies, the carbon locked up in it will be released into the atmosphere. What this means in practice is that atmospheric warming will suddenly accelerate.[24, 25] In Western Siberia, the massive frozen peat bogs, which cover an area the size of France and Germany combined, are starting to thaw. The once featureless expanse of frozen peat is turning into a landscape of lakes. Until now, billions of tons of marsh gas, or methane, have been locked up in the frozen bog. Methane is a greenhouse gas like carbon dioxide, but it is twenty times more potent. As the bog melts, it will release its methane into the atmosphere, again accelerating global warming.[26]

Knowledge of these feedback effects is recent, and so they have not been taken into account in climate-change predictions. As understanding grows, scientists are beginning to fear that changes such as those in the Amazon rainforest and Siberian bog could make global temperatures increase even faster than so far predicted. There may be a series of 'tipping points', or thresholds, where the responses of biological systems to man-made rises in global temperatures trigger even greater temperature change.

The only feasible way to avoid the disastrous effects of climate change is to make very large cutbacks in the amount of carbon dioxide we emit into the atmosphere. Many scientists and government bodies, including the UK Royal Commission on Environmental Pollution, have suggested that we should not allow atmospheric carbon dioxide to rise above 550 parts per million (compared to pre-industrial levels of 270 parts per million and current levels of 370 parts per million). However, others believe that in order to reduce the risk of unpredictable runaway effects we should not exceed levels of 450 parts per million, or even that we need to get atmospheric carbon dioxide levels down to about 350 — below current levels. All of these figures imply huge cutbacks in the rate at which we burn fossil fuels.

The most promising basis for a long-term agreement between countries is to allocate emissions rights on a per capita basis—that is, to allow equal shares per person, set at such a level that we do not exceed unsafe atmospheric concentrations of carbon dioxide. The Global Commons Institute developed the idea of 'contraction and convergence', which is probably the only politically realistic way of getting developing countries like China and India to agree to limit their carbon dioxide emissions. 'Contraction' involves first agreeing what level of atmospheric carbon dioxide is safe, and then working out by how much we must reduce worldwide emissions in order to stay below this level. 'Convergence' is a period of adjustment over several decades, during which nations' carbon quotas converge to the same per capita amount.[27] Using this framework, it is possible to calculate by how much carbon dioxide emissions in Britain must be cut. If 450ppm of atmospheric carbon dioxide is taken as the 'safe' level, our emissions must be reduced by 80 per cent, to a fifth of current levels, by 2050. Even if 550ppm were accepted as the safe level, emissions will still have to be cut by 60 per cent, and this is the figure currently accepted by the UK Government.

Within countries, the researcher Mayer Hillman has argued that there should be carbon rationing for individuals, in the same way that food and clothing were rationed during the Second World War, but with some 'trading' allowed, so that people leading more carbon-wasteful lifestyles could buy permits from more thrifty individuals.[28]

In the long term, it is possible that hydrogen fuel-cell vehicles will provide a carbon-dioxide-free car. However, this will depend on us having plentiful renewable energy from wind and wave power to produce the hydrogen fuel in the first place, and within the next 30 to 40 years it is likely that we will need all the renewable energy we can produce for domestic and industrial uses, with none left over to produce zero-emission hydrogen. In the short term, you can reduce carbon dioxide emissions from your car by choosing a smaller car, or buying a hybrid (electric plus fossil fuel) vehicle like the Toyota Prius or Honda Civic, but this will only reduce carbon dioxide emissions per mile travelled by about a third. To reduce transport-related carbon dioxide emissions by 80 per cent, you would still have to cut your car mileage by 70 per cent, even if you also changed from an ordinary car to a hybrid. In any case, any benefit achieved from people driving more fuel-efficient cars will be cancelled out if other people continue to buy more cars and use them more often to drive further. The most effective way to reduce carbon dioxide from travel is to drive less.

Objection 8: More traffic means more roads—means more traffic

The growth in traffic provides a spurious justification for the Government and local councils to spend billions of pounds on damaging new road schemes. Unfortunately, this leads to a vicious circle: as new roads are built, or existing roads and motorways are widened, they fill up with extra traffic, and quickly become as congested as roads which have not been widened.

The classic demonstration of this phenomenon was a study of the Westway, a 4-kilometre stretch of elevated motorway in west London which was opened in July 1970. Although the study was carried out a long time ago, it is still the most detailed analysis of what really happens (as opposed to what the planners predict will happen) when a new road is built.

John Elliott, a planner with the Greater London Council at the time, was responsible for the before-and-after analysis of traffic volumes on the Westway and the roads parallel to it, compared with other corridors into central London. He collected traffic-flow data, and was able to show how traffic volumes on the Westway soared in the four months after it opened. Although some of the cars using it had transferred from parallel roads, there were an extra 17,100 vehicles every day that could not be accounted for. They seemed to have come from nowhere. Within months, a third of the traffic on the newly built motorway was composed of drivers on completely new trips which had not been made by car before the road was opened.

Over the next five years, traffic on the Westway carried on growing much faster than on similar routes into London that had not been 'improved'. Between 1970 and 1975, traffic in the Westway corridor (that is, the Westway itself and parallel roads that drivers could use for similar trips) grew by 79 per cent. John Elliott compared the figures for the Westway with other road corridors into London: the Finchley Road corridor, to the north of the Westway, and the Old Brompton Road corridor to the south. He found that traffic did not grow at all on the Finchley Road corridor, and only by 1.5 per cent on the Old Brompton Road corridor.

By 1975, the vast majority (more than three-quarters) of the traffic using the Westway was additional car trips which had previously been made by public transport, or had not been made at all. The rapid growth of traffic on the Westway only ceased after 1975, when it had become as congested as the other roads. In other words, its construction had stimulated more car trips than would otherwise have been made. The individual reasons for all of those extra car trips are quite subtle: some people probably decided that it was now quicker to drive to their office in the morning than to catch the bus or tube; others made a trip that they would not have made before, for example deciding to take a new job which was now within driving distance, whereas before they might have looked for a job closer to home. Changes like this probably happened quite quickly. Over a longer timescale of a few years, other effects would have started to come into play, such as new development along or near the Westway, attracted there because the managing directors liked the prospect of being able to drive into work. The result of all these individual and quite subtle personal decisions was a huge increase in traffic noise (audible over a large area because the road was elevated) and traffic pollution.

John Elliott gathered similar evidence to show that new road building had generated large increases in traffic on five more routes around London: the M11 motorway; that part of the M25 which had already been built at the time he was writing; the North Circular Road; the Blackwall Tunnel; and the A316 near Heathrow Airport. His research was completed in 1985, and was submitted by the Greater London Council to the government of the day to try to persuade them to pull back from a large-scale road-building programme in London and across the UK.

However, his clear, simple logic and powerful evidence was rejected and the report was buried. It did not see the light of day again for another fourteen years, when it was published in full in an academic journal.[29] The journal's editor, Professor John Whitelegg, commented, "The high quality scientific information was not only ignored, it was deemed to be wrong.

Government had an ideologically based policy that majored on roads, and nothing as inconvenient as evidence was to be allowed to get in the way."

And this has been the problem for the last 40 years or more. Governments come and governments go, but sooner or later (generally sooner) each one of them decides to spend billions of pounds on bypasses, relief roads, development routes, distributor routes, regeneration roads, spine roads, radial roads, ring roads, link roads, access 'improvements', environment enhancements (!), gateway bridges, corridor improvements, motorway widening or some such. The names are different, but the effect is the same: to allow more vehicles to travel at higher speed to more out-of-town superstores or multiplex cinemas or business parks. As I write, in April 2005, the campaign network Road Block estimates that at least 200 such road schemes are planned across Britain.

As well as costing billions and encouraging extra traffic, road schemes destroy beautiful landscapes and tear apart communities. Despite the now overwhelming evidence that any short-term benefits to traffic flow are quickly eroded by traffic generation, big business and motoring organisations are still backing new road schemes, and politicians are still prepared to ignore the evidence set in front of them. There are so many examples that it is hard to know where to start in describing them, but let us look at one that has recently been approved by the Scottish Executive, the M74 Northern Extension in Glasgow.

This proposed extension is a five-mile stretch of six-lane elevated motorway that will run into the centre of Glasgow. In many ways, it looks similar on the map to the 1970s Westway in London, which is not all that surprising since the idea of extending the motorway network through this part of Glasgow goes back to city highway plans of the 1960s. Understanding of the effects of urban motorways has grown a great deal since then, and yet, strangely some might say, the idea for an urban motorway network has lived on in Glasgow, despite the fact that it is a city with lower than average car ownership and the potential for excellent public transport.

In 2005 the motorway was forecast to cost between £375 million and £500 million, although there were suggestions that this could rise to £1 billion because of difficulties with land contaminated with poisonous chromium wastes along the route. If the road costs £1 billion, this will be equivalent to about £120,000 per metre of road, making it one of the more expensive road schemes in Britain.

The M74 extension is highly controversial. It is opposed by a coalition of community and environmental groups, Joint Action against the M74, or JAM74 for short. Local residents are worried about the extra noise; the extra traffic that will be sucked into their communities in order to access the motorway; the greater danger caused by the additional traffic; the health risk from disturbing the poisonous chromium waste; the visual intrusion caused by a motorway on columns; the likelihood that the land underneath the motorway columns will attract muggers and criminals; and the barrier the motorway will form between houses and local shops and services, which will have to be reached by walking underneath the motorway itself. The area through which the motorway will pass is already quite desolate and run-down, as it has been blighted for decades by the possibility of motorway building.

In 1999, the Scottish Executive told the city council to go back to the drawing board and think again about alternative transport solutions, because of the likelihood that the road would encourage thousands more car commuters into central Glasgow. But no alternatives to the motorway were ever looked at. Instead, just over a year later, following heavy lobbying from the council and business organisations, the Scottish Executive changed its mind, and agreed to contribute towards the cost of the road.

A public inquiry followed. Usually, public inquiries are rubber-stamping exercises. It is almost unheard of for them to recommend against building a road scheme. But in this case, everyone was in for a surprise. The public inquiry sat for three months, with Richard Hickman and Donald Watt, the Inquiry Reporters, hearing evidence from objectors and supporters of the scheme. At the end of the hearings, they retired for four months to consider the evidence they had heard and to write their report. When it came, it was a bombshell. It concluded that the road scheme should not go ahead, because any benefits were outweighed by the disadvantages. It pointed out that the motorway would encourage increased traffic and more emissions of carbon dioxide; that the money could be better spent on public transport; and that there would be very serious adverse impacts on the environment of the local community. It concluded: "The proposal would be very likely to have very serious undesirable results; and . . . the economic and traffic benefits of the project would be much more limited, more uncertain, and (in the case of the congestion benefits) probably ephemeral."[30]

And that, you might think, would be the end of the story. The powers-that-be had looked into the evidence for and against the motorway in great detail for some seven months, hearing the opinions of all sides, and

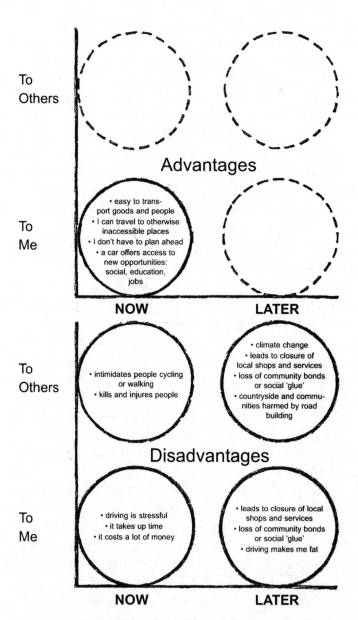

Figure 3: The advantages and disadvantages of cars.

had come to the view that this was an outdated, damaging road scheme which should not go ahead.

But, of course, it was not the end of the story. It is not possible to know what furious lobbying ensued after the publication of the inquiry report, but we can infer that the supporters of the scheme did not take this blow lying down. Eight months later, in March 2005, the Transport Minister, Nicol Stephen, announced that the M74 extension would, after all, go ahead. Remarkably—it is hard not to wonder whether he is really talking about the same project—Mr Stephen told the Scottish Parliament that "This is an important transport project and will bring much needed economic, social and safety benefits. It will improve the quality of life for local communities. It will reduce congestion on the M8 and local roads. It is also expected to reduce road injury accidents by up to 50 a year by removing traffic from local roads . . .The Public Local Inquiry Reporter recommended that the project should not proceed. However, Ministers concluded that the Reporter had not given enough weight to the positive aspects of the scheme as presented in evidence at the inquiry . . .This project is a key element in completing the central Scotland motorway network. We believe that the benefits of this project outweigh the disadvantages and that it is in the public interest to proceed."[31]

So there it is, and it feels that little has changed between the building of the Westway into central London in 1970 and the building of the M74 extension into central Glasgow nearly forty years later.

* * *

Writing about the damage caused by car culture, I feel conscious of the common jibe, "Oh, you're just anti-car." So it is necessary to reiterate that the car has benefits, as well as the disadvantages explored in this chapter. While the benefits are immediate and obvious, some disadvantages only become apparent decades later, and so the arrow connecting cause and effect is longer and less clear to see. The benefits are all now and for me, whereas the disadvantages are both now and later, and to me and others.

The car is an individualising technology, which encourages us to make self-interested choices and adopt self-centred values. Our car-oriented culture makes individuals feel that they have a right to enjoy the immediately obvious benefits of car use, while ignoring or denying the longer-term disadvantages to themselves and other people. We are offered instant satisfaction, and feel we are entitled to grab it. "I've got a right to drive my car where I want, when I want," some people say.

My argument is not that we must give up cars altogether. Rather, it is that our society should develop some self-restraint. We have to take responsibility for our actions. This is not altruism; it will be good for us as individuals as well as for others.

The twentieth century was the century of the car. The future can, if we want, be different. It is our choice. The engineers of the 1950s thought that they were building a car utopia, but what has been achieved is a car dystopia. Now we have to find a way forward from that dystopia, to a place where we are more discriminating about our car use, enjoy the benefits more selectively, and regain some of the quality of life that car culture has destroyed. It is, perhaps, a sign of the way cars have come to dominate our thinking that the best way I can describe this book is as a road map for that journey.

Chapter 3

Soft, small, stubborn: principles of de-motorisation

Paul Wynne works for the National Trust, managing their properties in Bristol and Bath. One of the properties in his care is a fine garden, Prior Park, on the outskirts of Bath. It has only been opened to the public fairly recently, but it is a great success story, with the number of visitors growing by nearly a third last year. However, it is a success story that might never have happened. When the National Trust first looked at opening the gardens to the public in the mid-1990s, local residents were up in arms. They had visions of hordes of visitors arriving, clogging the roads with traffic and parked cars. Paul Wynne says, "Our neighbours associated the National Trust with lots of cars and car parks. It soon became clear that there was nowhere to put a car park, and that anyway it would be extremely unpopular. So our PR offensive kicked in. The Trust declared it would adopt a sustainable transport approach, and run the gardens without a car park. We really didn't have any choice."

That decision was a radical one for an organisation which, across Britain, has more than 13 million visitors to its stately homes and gardens every year, 90 per cent of whom come by car. The Trust depends for its income on people being able to get to its properties, and cutting off the option of driving to Prior Park was like cutting off the blood supply to part of the Trust's corporate body.

Since the day the Trust made that decision, Paul and his colleagues have done everything they can think of to attract people to Prior Park on foot or by bus. They face quite a challenge: the garden is a thirty-minute walk from the centre of Bath, up a steep hill. They built a pull-in for buses outside the main gate of the property, and started paying the local bus company to provide extra services on Sundays, to tie in with opening and closing times. They persuaded an open-top tour bus company to start a tour route which included Prior Park. They paid for fingerpost signs to Prior Park, to help pedestrians find their way to the garden from the centre of the city. They swamped tourist information centres with a 'How to get to Prior Park landscape garden' leaflet, with a simple walking map and details of the bus services. The message of the leaflet is that the normal way to travel to the garden would be by foot or by bus. There is parking for cyclists at the garden, and the visitor kiosk looks after panniers and cycle helmets for people arriving by bike.

Initially doubtful, the local council only gave temporary planning permission for three years. The local ward councillor was sceptical. Paul faced the risk that he might have to close the gardens if he could not prove that they were operating successfully without swamping the area with traffic. But at the end of the three years, it was clear that the experiment had paid off. The feared traffic chaos had not materialised, the ward councillor was won over and the planning permission was made permanent with no opposition from local residents. The latest figures (for 2004) show about two-thirds of visitors to Prior Park walk, take the bus or cycle. Slightly less than a third come by car but park elsewhere, or are dropped off at the garden by car. Prior Park has not reduced its dependency on cars altogether, but they are a minor mode of transport instead of being the dominant one.

Paul Wynne is not rosy-eyed about the approach they have taken. "There has been some talk about using the car park that belongs to Prior Park College, at the top of the hill, during the summer. There's no doubt that if we had a car park we could double our numbers. But the staff at the garden aren't keen. They feel it would compromise our principles. Our aggressive marketing last year really paid off—we increased the number of visitors from 15,000 to 20,000. I don't believe we need a car park. We just have to be prepared to work harder to attract people."

There are two lessons from Prior Park. The first is that people's travel choices are more variable than sometimes assumed, and that it is possible to change them. The people who come to Prior Park are similar to those who go to other National Trust gardens, and when they go to other gardens most of them probably drive. But at Prior Park, it seems normal to walk or ride on the tour bus, so they do. The second lesson is that the things that make a difference may be quite small—an extra bus stop, a few signs. They may even require no tangible improvements at all, but simply involve telling people about the choices available. This chapter is about these techniques for influencing travel behaviour towards more environmentally friendly modes of transport—what are sometimes called the 'small-scale' and 'soft' ways of changing people's travel choices.

Broadly speaking, car trips follow what I think of as the 40:40:20 rule. Forty per cent of the car trips made by the average person could have been made by bike, foot or public transport without any new bus services or cycle tracks, or any other physical changes to streets and public transport. There was no reason for driving, apart from habit. Another 40 per cent are too far to walk, are difficult to cycle, and there is no bus or train service. For now, there is no option apart from driving, but the trip is such that it could be made by one of these modes if non-car options were improved. The last 20 per cent of trips have to be made by car—maybe there is a heavy load to be carried, or an elderly relative needs a lift.

These figures should not be taken too literally. They are order-of-magnitude estimates only, not precise calculations. The point they make is that the proportion of trips for which a car is essential is generally a lot smaller than people suppose; and the proportion for which a reasonably good 'green' alternative already exists is much larger than commonly supposed.

'Soft' is the name for the solutions that can influence the first 40 per cent of car trips. For these trips, there is no need to change things on the ground—there is already a fair choice. But the habitual driver doesn't know about the regular bus from the end of her road to the office, or thinks it is too old and dirty and slow. She might take the bus, but only if someone suggests it and gives her the right information about when it goes and how long it takes. The first trip may be the last if the bus is as bad as she thought, but if it is clean, quiet, safe and comfortable, she'll use it again. 'Soft' ways of cutting traffic deal with all these gritty problems. They pay attention to the quality of the journey. Are the buses smart? Are they comfortable with clean windows? Is the driver good with the passengers? Do they run on time? Next, do people actually know about the bus routes that travel where they are going? And what sort of image does bus travel have— dowdy and depressing, or smart, modern and efficient? Soft interventions are half about psychology and marketing, and half about listening to what your potential passengers say they want, and providing it. They can achieve a lot of change for very little money, and they can do it quickly.

The next 40 per cent can be influenced through 'small-scale' solutions. These car trips are tougher to tackle than the first group. They go to places where no bus or train runs, or late at night when the buses have stopped, or perhaps the journey could be made by bike but the only way there is on a main road which is too frightening to cycle. To affect these car trips, hundreds of small changes are needed, spread throughout city, suburbs and countryside: cycle parking spaces and networks of cycle lanes; door-to-door shared taxi-buses (a cross between buses and taxis); more frequent buses and trains on main routes; and good connections between all of these. There is no need to build big and costly new infrastructure, but to be effective these small changes must be spread everywhere: small-scale but writ large.

Finally, there are the 20 per cent of trips that are stubborn. Cars are ideal to collect pots of paint and wallpaper from the DIY shop on a Saturday morning, or to take grandparents out to tea in the country. These are sensible things to do with a car: important trips that could not be made any other way.

That 40:40:20 split might sound surprising. It seems hard to believe that it might be true—so many unnecessary car journeys! But here are a few examples that back it up, from Perth in Western Australia, three towns in England, and rural Wales, mostly places where you might think there are few alternatives to driving.

Perth is a sprawling city, where about eight out of ten trips are made by car. In 1997 the Western Australia Government commissioned a travel survey from a German company called Socialdata, which had built up a reputation for targeted marketing campaigns to get people out of cars and onto buses in several European cities. In preparation for a similar campaign in Perth, Socialdata carried out a travel survey, asking people why they had chosen a particular mode of transport for each trip. They were able to differentiate between people's subjective and objective reasons for choosing to drive. For example, a subjective reason might be that the interviewee did not know about the bus service that went where he wanted to go, or believed (incorrectly) that there was no service. An objective reason would be that there really was no adequate bus connection, or the interviewee had a heavy parcel to carry.

Socialdata managing director Werner Brög found that many of the car trips could have been made another way. For about 43 per cent, the only reasons for not walking, cycling or using public transport were subjective. A perfectly good alternative already existed. For about 39 per cent, improvements to the transport system were needed before a switch could be made—perhaps the provision of an adequate bus connection or better walking and cycling facilities. There were objective reasons for driving, but something could be done to help resolve them. For only 19 per cent were the alternatives out of the question—perhaps because someone was carrying a heavy load, or because they needed the car for their business.[1] Roughly speaking, the 40:40:20 split held true.

So much for sprawling suburban Perth. Might the same sort of pattern hold true in Britain?

Socialdata did a similar exercise to the one they had carried out in Perth, but this time in three English towns: Darlington, Worcester and Peterborough.[2,3] In each town, they asked 4,000 people to record their daily trips in a travel diary. Then they held hour-long interviews in the homes of 400 of the diarists, asking them in detail about the trips recorded in their travel diaries. Could the trips have been made by public transport instead of by car? Would it have been possible to cycle? They also asked about all sorts of factors that might have influenced people's choice: whether they believed the journey would be slower by bus; comfort; cost; whether they felt safe walking or cycling. Finally, the researchers went away and pored over public-transport timetables and cycle route maps, to find out how closely the perceptions of their interviewees matched reality.

In all the towns, at least a third of people's trips were already on foot, by cycle or by public transport. This is important in itself. Traditional transport consultants generally ignore the trips that people make on foot, and as a result their surveys overstate the significance of motorised travel.

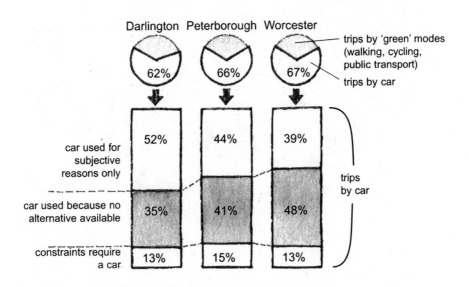

Figure 4: Trips by car and 'green' modes of transport.

That left two-thirds of the trips, which were made by car. Looking just at the car trips, the numbers tell a similar story to Perth. For between 39 and 52 per cent of car trips, the decision to drive had been made for entirely subjective reasons. There was already a bus service at about the right time, or the trip was short enough to walk or cycle and there was a safe route. For between 35 and 48 per cent, there was no alternative option available. Finally, between 13 and 15 per cent had to be made by car because of practical constraints. No matter how good the alternatives, these trips would always be in a car. Werner Brög described these trips in this way: "If your grandmother has a broken arm and you need to take her to hospital, nobody would expect you to go with her on the bus. You take the car."

Socialdata also worked out how far people travelled, and Werner Brög was struck by how short most of the car journeys were. In Darlington, nearly nine out of ten car trips within the city were less than 5 kilometres, so short that they could easily be cycled. Many were short enough to walk. These figures do not count car trips made outside the city, such as long dis-

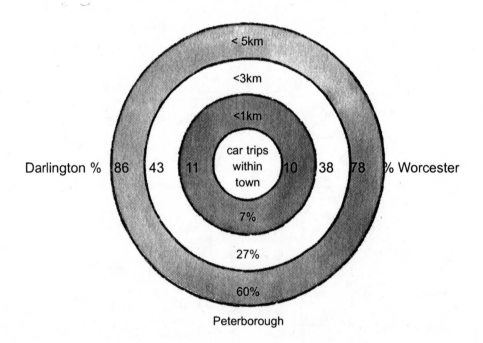

Figure 5: Car trip lengths in towns.
(based on survey data supplied by Werner Brög, Socialdata)

tance journeys on holiday or day trips to the countryside. But it is clear that almost all the car traffic in Darlington is caused by people whizzing around on very short journeys. Werner commented: "If you look at these short car trips, it becomes extremely difficult to believe they all have to be made by car. It becomes very clear there must be potential for change."

There was the same pattern in Worcester and Peterborough, although not quite so dramatic. The numbers in figures 4 and 5 tell an important story. They show that for most people living in these three towns—or, indeed, in any small to medium-sized town in Britain, since these three towns are in no way unusual—it is possible to do most everyday errands without using a car at all, but by foot or bike. Of course, this assumes that you are healthy and fit enough to walk a couple of miles, or cycle 3 miles. Still, it highlights the huge potential for walking and cycling, instead of driving, if only we could create an environment that was conducive to travel in this way.

When I first saw the results of Werner Brög's surveys, I was fascinated. But still, there was a niggling question. The data offered seemingly conclusive evidence that in towns, at least, there is great potential to cut car use by influencing people's attitudes and habits, but what about in the countryside? In the area of mid-Wales where I live, it is common for people to say things like "Oh, you have to have a car if you live round here—there's no other way to get around." It is assumed that a car is absolutely essential to rural life, and even people who think of themselves as environmentalists use a car as their prime means of transport. If it is true that a car is essential in rural areas, the 40:40:20 pattern we have seen in Perth, Darlington, Worcester and Peterborough breaks down.

In the villages around my home town of Machynlleth, I carried out a survey of people's travel patterns with Nat Taplin, a friend and fellow long-time transport campaigner. We gathered data on how people travelled for their everyday journeys, including trips to work by 250 people. Just over two-thirds of trips to work were by car. We found that these car trips did indeed seem to follow something close to the 40:40:20 pattern, although on the face of it the results were slightly more complicated.[4] For about a third of the car trips (34 per cent), a good alternative to the car was already available. Either the trip was short enough to cycle or walk along a safe route, or there was a public transport service from home to work which arrived at about 9 am and left between 5 pm and 6 pm. People were driving for subjective reasons. About a quarter of the trips (25 per cent) were

difficult by public transport or bike, but some fairly simple changes would
have made a difference, such as bus services arriving at about 9 am in the
morning, return tickets that could be used on either the bus or the train,
and cycle paths on the busy high-speed main road between two villages and
the town. For the next share of the trips to work (it came to 21 per cent),
public transport was not viable as the trips were from small villages away
from the main public transport routes, but car-sharing was an option, and
someone living nearby was already making the same car journey. All that
was needed was a car-share matching scheme to put people in touch with
each other, plus perhaps an incentive or bonus for those who took it up.
Finally, 20 per cent of the commuting trips really had to be made by car.
They were on complex cross-country routes that no bus would ever serve,
and there was no potential car-share partner travelling the same way.

Put all of those numbers together, and they do not exactly add up to
40:40:20. But if you treat the potential car-sharers as people who needed
an extra service—a car-share matching database rather than an extra bus,
but nevertheless something new—then the figures start to look familiar:
34 per cent who already have a good alternative but are not using it; 46
per cent for whom some small changes would make a difference; and 20
per cent of stubbornly car-dependent trips. Even in rural areas, it seems,
there could be huge potential for influencing people's travel choices.

Nat Taplin, the friend and colleague who worked with me on the travel
survey, has a practical streak. No pie-in-the-sky grandiose schemes—he
looks at what can be done right now to make people's travel options a bit
greener. He edits a regular guide to getting around the area by public
transport, which takes the indigestible public transport timetable books
produced by the two neighbouring county councils and boils them down
into one simple sheet that covers all the trips most people are likely to need
to make in our area. He also produces a little credit-card sized timetable
for the people who live in his village, Upper Corris, summing up the bus
times to and from Machynlleth. Initially he did it for himself, but he found
it so useful that he made lots of copies and dropped them through everyone's front door. It is a small thing to do. Nat says he did it partly for self-
ish reasons, because he wants the buses to be well used. But lots of his
neighbours keep the credit-card timetable in their wallets and purses. As
one said, "I couldn't understand the big timetable, but this is so much easier. Now all I need is that little card." Nat told me: "People carry it round
with them, and some have asked for another copy for their husband or

wife. If there was something like this for all the villages with a decent bus service, it would be a very cost-effective way of getting more passengers because it helps people understand what services are actually on offer." That, really, is the point. Small, simple changes can make a big difference, in the countryside as well as in the town.

* * *

It is one thing to spot the potential for car trips to be made by bus or foot or bike, but quite another to persuade people actually to make the change. Some subjective reasons for driving instead of catching the bus are strongly held and difficult to influence. One afternoon I met Werner Brög in Darlington to talk about how far marketing, information and persuasion could alter travel habits for the 40 per cent of car trips where an alternative is already available. "Look at all the trips in Darlington that are being made by car, even though they don't have to be," I said. "Surely there's no chance of persuading all those people to switch?"

Werner shook his head. "In cities like Darlington, I would say maybe a quarter of the trips where a car is used for subjective reasons are really easy to change, and another quarter is achievable. Then it becomes difficult. But that is the present situation. Once we achieve that first change, the community climate will also change. If people start cycling more, or using the bus more, the council will build better cycle lanes and the bus company will improve its bus service. And then it will be easier for other people to change. We live in a dynamic world."

Werner's story is an interesting one. He spent twenty years trying to persuade politicians and public transport companies to influence people's travel decisions by using marketing techniques. At the time, few politicians cared very much about the problem of rising traffic volumes, and those who did thought that the only solutions were to provide more public transport services, which they could not afford, or to increase petrol prices, which the public would not like. Werner was a maverick. He thought there might be another way, but no one believed him.

"I have no transport background," he told me. "I'm a behavioural scientist. I started my own market research company, Socialdata, in 1972. Our first project was on travel and we found 50 per cent of people who could use public transport didn't know about it. I found that very interesting."

He reasoned that it was cheaper, quicker and easier to tell someone about a public transport service they did not know existed, but which served the route they took, than to invest in a brand new public transport service for someone who had no bus passing their front door. If half of people did not even know about the services on offer, surely there was a great opportunity to increase public transport use, and at the same time increase ticket revenue to the bus and rail companies.

"I thought, this result is great, but for ten years I presented it and audiences laughed at me. And for the next ten years they realised it must be true but there was no idea they should do something about it. Then in Kassel in Germany we were using a panel of people for market research. We asked them questions about all sorts of things, again and again, and by the seventh time we came back to them, I felt we must give them an incentive or they'll get fed up. It happened that the next survey was about public transport, so I asked the public transport company if they would give us free tickets."

In return for the free tickets, Werner promised to do a follow-up survey of the panel members, to see if their travel patterns had altered. "We didn't expect much change—but it was a great effect. Then we did a similar piece of work in Nürnberg, and had some success. And then the boss of the Kassel public transport company had some money left over and said he would give it to us for a really good campaign. And that was the first individualised marketing campaign." In Kassel, use of public transport among the households targeted by the marketing campaign more than doubled.

Following the project in Kassel, Werner ran marketing campaigns to promote public transport, walking and cycling in towns and cities in Europe, Australia and America. Again and again, he found people cut their car driving and increased their travel by bus, train, foot and bike following his marketing campaigns. He called the work "individualised" marketing because people were given information that was tailored to their personal needs.

It might seem surprising that people can be persuaded to use their cars less, and public transport more often, just by giving them better information. Surely most of us are intelligent enough to work out for ourselves what is the most convenient way of making a particular journey? If it really was cheaper and quicker and more relaxing to walk or catch the train, and not to drive, surely we would do it?

The problem is that many people consistently remember public transport as worse than it actually is, and remember car travel as better than it actually is. Every time they plan a journey, they apply a distorting filter to the decision-making process. They are overly pessimistic about how long the trip will take by bus, and whether the bus will be on time. They concentrate their thoughts on the negative aspects of travelling by train, like the possibility that they will miss a connection. They think of how long it will take to walk to the shops. At the same time, they are overly optimistic about driving, assuming that the journey will be quicker than it really is, and concentrate on the positive feelings linked to car travel, like independence and flexibility, instead of the negative experiences, like traffic jams. They also underestimate the actual cost of travelling by car.

In Darlington, Werner asked people how long they thought a particular journey would take if it was made by public transport, and how long a journey would take by car. He found that on average, people overestimated the public transport journey time by 70 per cent, so that, for example, they assumed a 20-minute trip would actually take 34 minutes. They under-estimated the journey time by car by 26 per cent, assuming a 20-minute trip would actually take 15 minutes. In another survey, this time in Germany, he found the same car-bias in people's perceptions of the cost of travel. People overestimated the cost of public transport travel by 21 per cent, and underestimated the true cost of car travel by 58 per cent.[5]

Werner believes that car advertising is partly to blame for this distorting filter. "The reason for these misperceptions is simple," he told me. "There's a market with different providers—car manufacturers, bus companies, train companies, bike shops, and so on. Only one of them does any marketing, and they are the most professional. Some people say a quarter of the price of a car goes into advertising and marketing. These companies would not spend this money if it didn't work. The car is always in a wonderful landscape with no other cars. It isn't surprising if that influences people." Marketing by car companies not only affects people's decisions about which car to buy, but their feelings about which form of transport to use on a daily basis. It also helps shape the cultural climate in which we all live, since it encourages us to associate all sorts of positive values with cars: sporty looks, luxury, power, freedom, independence, a safe cocoon for our family, and so on.

Soft solutions—that is, giving people practical information and a positive reason for using green alternatives to the car—counteract this pro-car bias in our culture. They replace the subliminal message 'Driving is always the best way to travel' with the message 'Sometimes it's OK to drive, but other times it's healthier and quicker to walk, or more relaxing to take the train.'

As we have seen, there are plenty of car trips which do not actually require a car, and for which good alternatives are already on offer. Werner Brög's marketing campaigns in Kassel and Nürnberg suggest that it is possible to entice some people to try these alternatives. But there is one final question: what proportion of car drivers is open to influence? To answer this question, we go back to where this chapter began, with the National Trust.

Car drivers were in a minority amongst the visitors to Prior Park, the National Trust gardens on the outskirts of Bath. However, more than nine out of ten visitors to other National Trust stately homes and gardens arrive by car. This was a worry to the people running the National Trust: their ruling council was concerned about the environmental impact of so many car trips, but at the same time the Trust relied on these visitors for its income, and did not want to deter people from coming. So they decided to commission some research, to find out how many of their visitors were thoroughly wedded to their cars, and how many might be open to other travel options.

The research was done by a psychologist, Jillian Anable. She carried out detailed surveys of over 600 visitors to two National Trust properties in the north-west of England, Quarry Bank Mill and Dunham Massey, asking about visitors' attitudes and values as well as their preferred mode of travel.[6] She found that the visitors divided quite neatly into six groups with different psychological profiles, which she nicknamed malcontented motorists, aspiring environmentalists, complacent car addicts, diehard drivers, carless crusaders and reluctant riders.

The first four groups all owned a car, but they had startlingly different attitudes to driving. The malcontented motorists felt guilty about using their car unnecessarily and frustrated at traffic congestion, and believed that they had a moral responsibility to use their cars less. They accounted for 30 per cent of the people questioned. The aspiring environmentalists did not particularly enjoy car travel and saw many negative aspects of car use, although they appreciated certain practical advantages of the car and were therefore reluctant to give up ownership entirely. They had already cut back on their car use, and intended to reduce further where they could. They formed 18 per cent of the people questioned.

The complacent car addicts had no such feelings. They could not see any problems with car use, and accordingly felt no reason for driving less. They were not particularly attached to their cars; it was just that they saw no need to behave differently. This group made up 26 per cent of those surveyed.

The diehard drivers were the only group that could be described as having a love affair with their cars. They enjoyed car travel, cared about what car they drove, and were more likely than the other groups to believe that all their car use was necessary. They felt strongly about an individual's right to drive a car. They made up 19 per cent of the total sample.

The remaining two groups did not own a car, but their reasons for this were different. The carless crusaders (4 per cent of the people surveyed) were very concerned about the environment and had positive perceptions of travel by alternative modes. The reluctant riders (the smallest group, at 3 per cent) were involuntary users of public transport, either because they could not afford a car or because they could not drive for health reasons. They were not much motivated by environmental issues, and would have liked to have greater access to a car, either hoping to own a car in the future or accepting lifts by car whenever possible.

Jillian Anable's research suggested that some types of people are much easier to influence than others. Among the car drivers, roughly half are hard nuts to crack, people whose minds it would be difficult to change. These are the diehard drivers and the complacent car addicts. But the other half, the malcontented motorists and aspiring environmentalists, have a different set of attitudes and values, and are easier to influence. The attitudes and opinions of the four car-owning groups largely cut across demographic differences like age, sex, employment status and income, although the malcontented motorists and aspiring environmentalists tended to be more highly educated than the diehard drivers and complacent car addicts. The lesson is clear—we may not be able to persuade everybody to abandon their car and take the bus or bike instead, but there are enough people who are receptive to doing this to make the effort worthwhile.

* * *

In this chapter we have established two important points, which are crucial to the argument in the next three chapters. The first point is that a good proportion of car trips could be made by more sustainable means. This is the 40:40:20 rule. Forty per cent of car trips could be made by sustainable means tomorrow, without any physical changes to the green alternatives; another 40 per cent require some improvements to public transport and walking and cycling facilities; and for 20 per cent a car is absolutely required and no alternative is feasible.

The second point is that as many as half of all car drivers are willing to change their travel behaviour. These people—the ones profiled by Jillian Anable as malcontented motorists and aspiring environmentalists—are psychologically receptive to the possibility of using their car less.

As figure 6 shows, there is a good proportion of car trips where soft or small-scale solutions could help the driver switch to a green mode and where the driver is willing to make the switch.

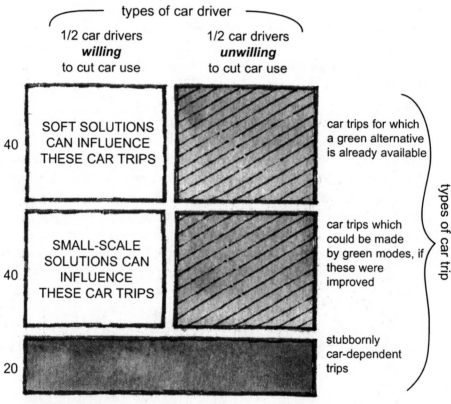

Shaded areas show car use that cannot be tackled, either because the *trip* is stubbornly car-dependent, or the *driver* is unwilling to change.

Unshaded areas show car use that can be tackled through soft and small-scale solutions.

Figure 6: The potential for change: types of car driver and types of car trip.

It is often said that we have a 'love affair' with the car, but Jillian Anable's research suggests that this is only true for a minority of people, and that most people are far more flexible in their travel decisions than might be imagined. The potential for soft and small-scale solutions to make a difference is therefore great. This is good news for the National Trust, wanting to find ways to reduce car trips to their stately homes without losing takings at the turnstile. It is also good news for the rest of us, as we turn now to look at practical examples of initiatives to seduce the psychologically receptive drivers out of the driving seat.

Chapter 4

Soft solutions to de-motorise the rush hour

Every weekday morning, Stan Ryan pulls on a bright yellow reflective coat and sets out with his two young children to walk the three-quarters of a mile to their school, St Sebastian's Roman Catholic Primary. The school is in inner-city Liverpool, on a residential street sandwiched between two noisy and polluted arterial roads. On the way they pick up other children as the procession passes their homes, so that by the time they turn into the school gate there is a cheerful gaggle of more than twenty children of all ages from four to eleven, all wearing bright yellow like Stan. Some days they are joined by Val Wright, who works at the school as a welfare assistant. On other days, parents or grandparents join the procession.

Val and Stan are among the thousands of parents and staff at primary schools across the country who have set up 'walking buses'. A walking bus is a fixed walking route to school, with special 'bus stops' to pick up children along the way. Just like a real bus, it runs to a timetable. It has a volunteer parent to act as 'driver' and another to be the 'conductor'. At St Sebastian's, there are three walking buses, which together have cut the number of children being driven to school by a third.

St Sebastian's was the first of four schools in Merseyside that I visited as part of a study for the Department for Transport.[1] We wanted to find out whether it is possible to break the habit of bundling the kids into the back of the car for the school run. The parents and staff there seemed to feel they had cracked it. Over tea and biscuits in the staff room, Stan, Val and the head teacher, Dennis Hardiman, explained the difference their work had made. "Hail, rain or snow, we've not once abandoned the walking bus," claimed Stan. "The children get to meet their friends. Sometimes we have singing. A lot of the parents are really up for it. And it's having an impact on the cars—they are backing off." Before the walking buses

Heavy school bags go on the trolley of the walking bus.

started, the road outside the school was clogged with cars at 8.50, and dangerous for the children. Now there are fewer cars, and those parents that still drive tend to park further away. Val felt the bus was good for the children's development: "It gives the children confidence and makes them streetwise with traffic. By Year Five they are allowed by parents to come to school by themselves. The walking bus prepares them. It gives them the independence and road safety skills and social skills."

On the other side of Merseyside, in leafy suburban Ainsdale, the head teacher of St John Stone Primary School was equally enthusiastic. Paul Conkling is a fitness fanatic; before taking up teaching he built racing bikes. Every week, his school has a 'Walking Wednesday' or a 'Fresh Air Friday' when the children are encouraged to walk to school, or at least part of the way. A large banner hangs on the wall by the school entrance: 'WALKING — next walk to school Wednesday 5 November'.

There were two new cycle shelters next to the front gate, full of children's bikes and a few scooters. All the older pupils at St John Stone receive cycle training—not just the old-style cycling proficiency test involving weaving round a few traffic cones on the playground, but proper off-road and then on-road training, so that they are confident cycling on real roads by the time they leave for secondary school. In the weeks running up to the cycle training, Paul Conkling runs a cycle maintenance session at Friday lunchtimes and afternoons. This is not just about changing brake-blocks and repairing a puncture. He grinned as he described it: "The children bring in their bikes, and we take one apart, right down to the ball-bearings." Once or twice a term there is a family cycle-to-school day, for which the children can borrow cycle helmets and fluorescent jackets if they need them.

The pupils are closely involved in running the school's walking and cycling schemes, and monitoring their effects. While we were talking, two pupils, Tom and Portia, came in to show us some graphs of how children had got to school the previous day, which was a Walking Wednesday. It had been a cold, miserable day with sleety rain, but 31 children had walked and five had cycled. Some other walking days, they said, the figures looked much better. Occasionally as many as 80 children walked.

Despite the work by Paul and the pupils, a lot of parents still drive. Paul seemed frustrated about this, but he is playing a long game: "We are trying to alter the mindset, so hopefully the children will continue to walk and cycle into adulthood. They know all about pollution. But it's taking a long time to get the parents to appreciate the reasons for what we're doing. The car has really spoiled our generation." It is not that the roads around the school are too dangerous; in fact its location looks ideal for walking or cycling. The problem lies in people's habits and the choices they make every day without a moment's thought.

Changing the choices made by parents is tough, but Paul has some back-up from a consortium of local councils across Merseyside, called Merseyside TravelWise. The TravelWise team is helping over 120 schools, about a fifth of the schools in the conurbation, to draw up what is known as a school travel plan. Dave Wells from TravelWise explained how he worked with the schools to get children out of cars. "We draw up an action plan for every school, which is agreed with the school in September and covers the whole year. The action plan covers things like when there will be special walking days or events like health weeks; and what resources we will supply to the school, such as posters and fliers. At least once a term, I meet the school to discuss how things are going. There is also a lot of less formal contact—for example, if there is a special cycle train on a particular day, I'll be there to support it. That's like a walking bus, but the kids come on their bikes. We offer a special school assembly about school travel—it's very interactive. And we attend parents' evenings."

The TravelWise team can also pay for installation of cycle shelters, or for changes to the streets around the school, such as traffic calming and zebra crossings. The cycle shelters at Paul Conkling's school were funded this way. At Val Wright's school, St Sebastian's, there was money for new street lights and a zebra crossing. Val felt this was a great leap forward: "Grandmas in this area have wanted a zebra crossing there for 39 years," she said. Dave Wells was also planning a 20mph speed limit and traffic calming, to stop drivers using the road past St Sebastian's as a rat-run to beat the traffic lights on the main road.

Dave Wells is one of a new breed of council officers, a school travel co-ordinator. He is approachable, casually dressed in a tracksuit and trainers, and he used to work with youth groups. Whereas the traditional traffic engineer can tell you in precise detail how to design a traffic junction, Dave's expertise is in communicating with people, getting everyone on the same side, working together.

Merseyside is doing well by its children, but it is by no means unique. From Kent to Cumbria, parents, teachers and that new breed of council officers are working together to break the habit of the school run. It is not an easy task—one school travel co-ordinator told me "every September it is a real battle. If there's a walking bus, there is lots of work to get the new parents and children on board." Despite the problems, it seems to be working. The evidence from the thirty schools we visited for the Department for Transport project, right across England, was that a good school travel plan can cut car trips to school by nearly a quarter, and that some schools can cut car use by as much as a half.

The most successful schools seem to be the ones where someone is really determined to change things. It could be a parent, a governor, a teacher, or a group of pupils. That special someone cajoles, pesters and enthuses everyone else, leading to a steady flow of walking and cycling days, articles in the school newsletter, special assemblies and prizes for children who have walked the most. Travel to school stays at the top of everyone's agenda.

Good support from the local council is also important. In one local authority, the school travel co-ordinator said that in the early days they had spent a lot of money on traffic calming around schools, but had not really bothered to check what the schools wanted first. The result: not much change. Then the council switched tactics. The schools were encouraged to set up walking buses and children were given prizes for regular walking to school. The council promised money for whatever each school felt was needed to get more pupils walking and cycling, but only if the school had itself done something to cut car use. Some schools asked for cycle shelters; others asked for what became known as gazebos—sheltered areas where parents could wait to pick up their children. Often, the schools asked for changes that were a lot simpler and cheaper than the council had expected. The result this time: a fifth less car driving on average.

The other lesson is that school travel plans work best when the pupils are closely involved in running them. After all, it is their journey to school. At Billinge Chapel End School in the Wirral, the third of the Merseyside schools I visited, teacher Marion Hobbs said, "Get the children fired up, so they nag you to do things!" She had found lots of ways of bringing school travel into the curriculum. Children designed fliers for a Walk on Wednesday campaign, looked at traffic problems outside the school as part of their geography lessons, did surveys and mapping to trace their routes to school and discussed whether they could walk together. "Gimmicks work well, to capture the children's imagination so they go home and talk about it. Like the Golden Shoe, a spray-painted shoe which is awarded to the class that has walked the most. Some of the children think it is real gold. If the children are fired up, they prick your conscience if not enough is going on. They also remember to fill in the wall charts in the cloakrooms to show how they have got to school, whereas teachers sometimes forget."

Both parents and children often say they would prefer not to travel to school by car. One survey found that 65 per cent of parents would prefer not to drive, but feel that they have no alternative.[2] Another survey asked children how they preferred to travel. It found that as children reach the upper years of primary school they want to walk or cycle to school: in Year Six only 8 per cent of the children questioned said that they wanted to travel by car, much less than the number who actually did so.[3]

The schoolchildren in Merseyside feel the same way. Debbie Dempsey, a learning mentor at Park Brow School in Knowsley, told me how popular walking to school was with their children. They set up two walking buses, which are timed to arrive at school just as the breakfast club starts. This means the children get some exercise, fresh air and then a healthy breakfast before they start school. Debbie commented: "The children thoroughly enjoy it. They want to sing, it's a much nicer way to start the day. The children on the school council recently met people coming in to look at the school, and were asked to choose four things to tell the visitors about. They chose the teachers, the dinners, the walking bus and the breakfast club. The children also designed the logo for the walking bus—

the Park Brow Travellers. Children in Year Six were heavily involved in developing the bus. They've now left, but when they come back they want to know how it's going." About 15 per cent of Park Brow pupils have used the walking bus at some stage, and many of those who previously travelled with the walking bus are now walking to school with their parents.

Walking to school makes children happy, but it also helps their educational development. At Park Brow, Debbie said: "The children who had difficulties not listening, or shouting—their teachers have commented how much calmer they are. And they are more organised because their mums aren't carrying everything for them—they are looking after themselves. There are at least three children whose behaviour was extremely challenging, and they are now much calmer. The children have had a chance to talk to their friends for an hour, so they are more settled." Debbie originally started the school's walking buses because she thought they could help improve the children's attendance and punctuality at school. "Some children were arriving half an hour late, having been dragged out of bed, with no breakfast, or having waited half an hour for a taxi. With the walking bus this has changed. Before, about forty to fifty children might arrive late; now this is down to ten or eleven."

There is another benefit from projects like these. Excessive car use is creating overweight children, who will grow into overweight adults. Professor Roger Mackett from University College London looked at physical activity amongst 10-13-year-olds in Hertfordshire, and found that walking or cycling to school—or even taking the bus—could make a big difference to the amount of physical activity a child got over the week.[4] Walking to school every day for a week used up more energy than two hours of PE and games lessons, the recommended standard. What is more, the children who walked to school were more active than their car-borne friends once they arrived. The 'walkers' burned more calories during PE, games and break time in the playground. Overall, they used nearly a third more calories on a wide range of activities than the car-borne kids.

Walking Wednesdays, Fresh Air Fridays, cycle trains and walking buses may be catching on at schools, but what about the parents? If mothers and fathers are still driving to work, school travel campaigns like those in Merseyside will not have much effect on rush hour traffic. After all, a lot of parents drop the kids off at school on the way to the office. So, let us look at some soft solutions to tackle the car trip to work.

* * *

Some surprising things have begun to happen. The pharmaceutical giant Pfizer has started to pay its employees £2 a day not to drive to work at their huge rural campus near the seaside town of Sandwich in Kent.[5] Faced with the choice of buying more land to build a bigger car park for their expanding staff or investing in other ways of getting employees to work, Pfizer decided on the second option. They calculated it was cheaper to pay people what they called 'parking cash out' of £2 per day. The calculation is clear-cut: each extra parking space would have cost up to £3,000 in construction, access roads and lighting, plus £500 every year for maintenance and staffing. If an employee takes the bus to work every day for a year, the 'parking cash out' only costs Pfizer £480.

With the money saved, Pfizer provided a free shuttle service for their staff from the town centre and railway station, running every ten minutes at the beginning and end of the day and during the lunch hour, and every twenty minutes during the rest of the day. They paid the local bus company to run extra services, including an evening bus service to Canterbury, where many employees lived. They contributed towards the cost of new cycle tracks between Sandwich and the nearby towns of Deal and Ramsgate. They also put a car-sharing database on the company intranet, which allowed employees to find possible car-share partners. The effect of these initiatives was to cut the number of cars arriving on site from 75 per 100 employees to 68 per 100 employees over two years—that is, a 10 per cent cut in car use. The Pfizer site is a big one, with more than 5,000 people working there every day. By encouraging employees to leave the car at home, Pfizer cut the demand for parking by about 400 spaces, saving nearly £1 million.

This type of initiative by an employer has become known as a 'workplace travel plan'. Hundreds of companies, big and small, are following Pfizer's lead. They are trying all sorts of ways of getting their employees to walk, cycle, take the bus or train or share the car trip with a colleague.

In Manchester, the Highways Agency took dramatic action to cut the number of car-borne commuters amongst their regional workforce. This might come as a surprise, because the agency is responsible for building new roads and motorways, and their staff might be expected to be more attached to their cars than most. However, over a six-year period from 1998 to 2004, they cut the number of people driving to the office in Manchester from seventy to about thirty. Pete Evans, the Highways Agency's national travel co-ordinator, told me their success was the result of a mix of carrots and sticks. People who travelled to work by train or bus got a 10 per cent discount on their season ticket and an interest-free loan. To help cyclists, the Highways Agency installed showers and lockers. Some staff were encouraged to work from home.

As part of city-centre redevelopment plans, the Highways Agency also cut the size of its car park. This might sound like an unpopular thing to do, but because it was linked with the other changes it was accepted by employees. Crucially, the agency made sure that the reduced number of spaces was allocated fairly. It promised that disabled people and car-sharers would be guaranteed a parking space. Pete Evans said: "We see car-park management as our number one priority to achieve a shift away from cars. Before we brought in the travel plan, there was intense pressure on the car park, and because we work flexitime it used to be full by 7 a.m.— mostly with cars belonging to senior male grades with no child-care responsibilities, who started work early to ensure they got a parking space. By guaranteeing spaces for car-sharers, we have made it easier for other staff, particularly women. If you can car-share, you know you'll be able to park. Now, the car park doesn't fill up till 9.30 a.m. Because we already had pressure on the car park, people were really into the idea of guaranteed spaces for sharers."

The mobile phone company Orange has been busy too, at their offices in Bristol. When the company moved some of its employees from an out-of-town business park to new city-centre offices close to the railway station, there was very limited space for car parking, with only some 100 spaces for 400 relocated staff. Like the Highways Agency, Orange brought in a parking permit system. Their staff score points based on whether they have child-care responsibilities; how easy it is for them to get to work by public transport, cycling or walking; whether they are contracted to work outside normal office hours; whether they are a car sharer; the number of trips offsite they need to make; and whether they have to transport heavy or awkward equipment. Permits are reissued every six months, and employees who do not have enough points to qualify for a parking permit are instead entitled to a monthly payment which is roughly equivalent to the cost of a public transport season ticket. Alongside the permit system, Orange made sure that it was easy for their staff to travel by other means. They paid for a shuttle bus, which runs every half-hour through the day between the new office and another office which is still on an out-of-town business park, so people could easily get to meetings with colleagues during the day. They made sure there was space for employees to park a bike, and showers and lockers for storage of cycle helmets, panniers and sweaty cycling gear. They offered an interest-free loan of up to £750 for buying a bike. They also set up a car-sharing scheme, under which they promised to pay for the cost of a taxi ride home if an employee's sharing arrangement fell through, for example because their work colleague had to leave early to sort out an unexpected problem at home.

The result was dramatic. When Orange had its office on the business park, 80 per cent of the workforce travelled to work by car. After they moved and brought in the workplace travel plan, only 27 per cent were still driving to work. These were the same people. The lesson is simple: facilitate car access by providing acres of tarmacked car park, and most people will drive; facilitate public transport access, and the same people will take the train or bus.

Pfizer, the Highways Agency and Orange have cut car commuting by their employees through a mixture of soft interventions—that is, giving people better information about travel options that already exist, and incentives to use them—and small-scale improvements, like showers and lockers for cyclists, or extra bus services at the right time in the evening. They have also been tough about car parking, either cutting the number of parking spaces or not adding parking when the size of their workforce grew.

But are these companies the exception rather than the rule—lucky in where they are located, and with employees who live conveniently close to bus routes? Will this type of project only work in places where there is already an excellent public transport network? It is all very well to cut back on parking spaces, but would this lead to employees parking off-site, on grass verges and other people's driveways?

In fact, there is evidence that what Pfizer, the Highways Agency and Orange have done can work anywhere. Whether an office, factory or call centre is in a suburban business park or surrounded by green fields, there is still the potential to cut the number of cars being driven to work. In California, hardly known for its high use of public transport, the researcher Donald Shoup reported that an incentive payments scheme like the one used at Pfizer had cut vehicle mileage for the commute to work at eight companies by an average of 12 per cent.[6] Californian law requires companies to offer their employees the choice of a cash payment instead of a parking space. In practice, many companies do not know about the law and it is not actively promoted or enforced, which is a pity, because amongst those companies that know about it the effect is clearly positive. Donald Shoup found that the scheme was popular with employees, because they got the choice of extra money equivalent to the value of their parking space; that it was simple and cheap to run; and that it was effective at cutting traffic.

Schemes like this succeed because many people could walk, cycle, take the bus or car-share to get to work, but have simply never thought about doing it. No one has ever asked them whether it might be attractive to have a few extra pounds in their bank account at the end of the month, instead of free parking. When asked, people are surprisingly willing to consider the alternative ways they could get to work and, even in difficult suburban or rural locations, can often identify several practical options. They may not be prepared to use those options every day of the week, but they do not need to. Even travelling by bus one day a week can help cut traffic, if others do the same.

The responses people make when asked to consider green travel options are illuminating. I asked employees at seven regional offices of a government agency whether they would be willing to travel to work by green methods, such as walking, cycling, public transport or car-sharing, at least some of the time. Most of the offices were on the edges of towns or in out-of-town business parks—that is, in locations that might be considered difficult to reach without a car. Yet the response from every office was positive. Typically, two-thirds of employees said that they would be willing to use environmentally friendly options for getting to work, at least sometimes. About half of those who drove could identify an alternative way of getting to work that would be easy for them personally. Most often, people felt that car-sharing was the easiest alternative, but many said it would be easy to cycle, and some said they could easily walk or catch the bus. Putting the two sets of figures together, more than four in every ten employees were willing to use non-car options and said they could think of an alternative which was practical for them. Even if these people only left the car at home a couple of days a week and drove the rest of the time, the offices could cut their car travel by nearly a fifth. These employees were not unusually 'green'. Their normal way of getting to work was by car, and in fact they were slightly more likely to drive to work than the UK average, probably reflecting the fact that most of the offices were in rural or suburban sites.

So far, we have looked at green ways of travelling to work. But there is another way of cutting back on car commuting, which is to work from home. This is not an option for everybody. It is unlikely to be a choice open to people who have a public-facing role, such as working on a reception desk or in a shop, or providing health care. If you are packing chickens for a supermarket or driving trains, you have to be there to do it. However, the number of jobs which include some 'location-independent' tasks, or tasks you can do anywhere, is increasing, largely because of email and the internet. Since the 1970s, pundits have been forecasting that telecommunications and information technology will transform our travel behaviour, without much sign that they are right, so a little scepticism on this might be understandable. But during the late 1990s, the number of people working from home 'at least one day a week using a telephone and a computer' (which is the Government's definition of teleworking) went up by an average of 13 per cent each year. There are now more than 2 million people in the UK who work from home some of the time, and there is no sign yet that the trend is slowing.

One of the companies to have led the way in encouraging staff to work from home is the telecommunications firm BT. In the early days, the company was interested in finding out whether teleworking could work—after all, as the biggest telecommunications company in the UK, BT had a lot to gain commercially if it did. But they were also interested in using their office space more efficiently. They discovered that the desks in their offices were only being used about 25 per cent of the time, and they started to wonder whether it might be possible for their staff to 'hot-desk'.

Now, so long as their manager agrees, BT employees can opt into a scheme called Workabout, which enables them to work from home. They get a computer and phone line installed at home, a budget for buying office furniture, the option of working some of the time at a telecentre close to their home, and access to help and advice if there are any problems. By 2003, about 7,500 employees were registered with Workabout, out of BT's workforce of slightly over 100,000.[7]

The effects of the BT scheme have been closely monitored, revealing a lot about the positive, and a few negative, effects of teleworking. The initiative cut the time the Workabout employees spent behind the steering wheel, even allowing for the fact that once they were not driving to work every day, some employees drove more for other trips—for example making a special journey to the supermarket whereas previously they would have picked up the shopping on the way home from work. Peter Hopkinson and Peter James, two of the researchers who monitored the scheme, measured typical net reductions in car mileage of about 180 miles per week for each teleworker, even taking account of these extra trips.[8,9,10]

As interesting as the mileage savings are the other things the teleworkers said about what it is like to work from home. The personal benefits were manifold. Nine out of ten teleworkers said they now had a better quality of life, and that working at home had positive effects for their partner or their children. Some said that since they no longer had an arduous commute to work, they had more time for activities in their local community. People talked about feeling less stressed, being able to have lunch with their children, and being able to help more with household tasks so that they spent more 'quality time' with their spouses. About half of the teleworkers said they had saved money as a result of working at home, with many reporting savings of over £1,000 a year. One in ten said that being able to work from home had enabled them to carry on doing a job that they would otherwise have had to leave. For example, one man said, "I am now able to take the kids to school and their other activities, which has been an absolute godsend as my wife has recently been diagnosed with MS."

Some people were less positive about teleworking, mainly saying it made them feel cut off from colleagues in the office, or that they missed the exercise associated with travelling to work: "Going downstairs for breakfast is as strenuous as it gets." However, the proportion with negative opinions was low, with only about 5 per cent saying they were dissatisfied.

Peter Hopkinson and Peter James found evidence that teleworking was good for BT, too. Eight out of ten of the teleworkers said working from home made it easier to concentrate, and that they were able to produce better quality and more creative work. Teleworking employees take less time off sick than their counterparts in the office, and the option of working from home means women are more likely to come back to work after maternity leave. Finally, the reorganisation of office space that BT was able to carry out as a result of its Workabout scheme contributed to large financial savings.

Earlier in this chapter, we met Dave Wells from Merseyside Travelwise, the man from the local authority who was helping schools to set up walk-to-school days and walking buses. In the same way that local councils have started talking to parents and headteachers about school travel, some are also fixing meetings with company chief executives to persuade them to imitate BT, Pfizer and Orange.

In Birmingham, I visited Mike Cooper and Helen Davies, who ran a project called Company TravelWise, whose aim is to make it easy for businesses and their employees to be green. Mike and Helen work in a tower block overlooking a spaghetti tangle of road junctions. From the city centre, you can walk to their office in about fifteen minutes. Ten years ago the first part of the walk was a tarmac and metal jungle, with guard rails corralling pedestrians into narrow spaces between the hooting cars. Now, Birmingham is more civilised, with more pedestrianised streets and some beautiful city squares. But the last few minutes walk are through unchanged 1960s Birmingham, a city where cars came first. Pedestrians must negotiate a subterranean network of tunnels, occasionally emerging into a well of light surrounded by the concrete pillars of aerial motorways, before ducking down into another tunnel. It is a reminder of what happens when you try to solve traffic congestion by building more roads.

Mike and Helen are trying to solve traffic congestion another way. Instead of tarmac and concrete, they are doing it by talking to people. Companies are invited to affiliate to Company TravelWise, and when I met them in summer 2003, more than 160 had already done so. Each company got whatever help it needed to set up a travel plan like those at Orange and Pfizer. Helen told me: "We do the legwork for them and offer a menu of options." Once a company joins, its employees are entitled to cut-price public transport passes if they give up their office parking space—a hefty 50 per cent off in the first year and 5 per cent per year after that. Helen and Mike send them public-transport timetables each time the bus and train services change. The companies get discounts on cycle parking stands. They also get personal help and advice to sort out specific transport problems faced by their staff. Mike said: "A lot of our role is sorting out problems. Any obstacle that gets in the way of someone being sustainable, we'll try to sort it out—whether it's cycle parking, street lighting, poor bus routes that don't meet shift patterns, or an access route from a business park to a station."

Mike and Helen's work is mirrored in Bristol, Cambridge, York and Nottingham. The different towns have tried many ways to get a foot in the door with company bosses. Nottingham offers grants to smaller businesses, to pay for the cost of cycle parking or car-sharing schemes. In Bristol and York, businesses that want to extend an office or factory are told that they must draw up a workplace travel plan or they will not be given planning permission. In Cambridge, the local council paid towards the cost of a new bus station at the town's hospital, Addenbrooke's, as part of a scheme to get hospital staff to work by bus. Nottingham and Bristol have set up 'green commuter clubs', in which businesses work together to encourage their staff to car-share or take public transport. For example, companies that had offices near the railway station in Nottingham linked up with the train company to promote commuting by rail to their employees.

Little by little, all this work is starting to take effect. During 2003 and 2004, I worked with colleagues from University College London, Robert Gordon University in Aberdeen and research company Eco-Logica to find out how much difference workplace travel plans and similar initiatives could make.[11] We talked to people like Mike Cooper and Helen Davies in seven towns to find out how they thought the companies in their towns were getting on. Some of them were able to point to impressive successes like Orange in Bristol, but there were also examples of businesses which had tried a bit but then given up, where there was little overall effect on people's commuting patterns. However, putting together the successful and the not-so-successful examples, businesses had on average cut the number of cars being driven to work by about a fifth (the exact figure was 18 per cent). Most businesses had cut car trips to work by 10-25 per cent; some had not cut car trips at all, and some had achieved cuts of a third or even more.

What are the lessons from this? First, that most people never stop to think about whether they could take the bus to work, share the car trip with a colleague, or cycle. But when actually asked, many people are surprisingly willing to consider one of these green alternatives. The greener options do not work for everyone, and they may not be convenient all the time, and that's fine. If you really do need your car to get to work, use it. But for many people, a cut-price season ticket or showers at work are enough to tip the balance in favour of bussing or cycling to work, and the accumulated effect of many people making small changes in their travel patterns—even just once or twice a week—is large. If every business had a workplace travel plan, there would be noticeably less rush hour congestion, with weekday morning traffic about the same as it is during the school summer holidays.

For years, businesses have paid the cost of parking spaces for their employees, offering what US researcher Donald Shoup called a 'matching grant' for driving to work. The employer pays part of the cost of the commute (the parking cost) only if the commuter pays the rest of the cost (the petrol). Not surprisingly, many employees—in fact, most of us—take up that grant. Considered purely from a self-interest perspective, we would be fools not to. What needs to change now is for employers' 'matching grants' to be designed to spur employees to walk, cycle, use public transport or car-share.

Exactly the same argument applies to getting the children to school. For some families, there really is no alternative to driving. But for many, a small incentive or a helping hand could tip the balance and make it easier, nicer or more fun to walk, cycle or catch the bus. This might be building a gazebo where parents can wait for their children in the dry, or providing cycle shelters, a zebra crossing or traffic calming, or offering a golden shoe to the class which walks the most.

The evidence from these schools and businesses is hopeful. For regular journeys to school and work, simple interventions can have far-reaching effects. If applied everywhere, these soft solutions could make the rush hour a lot less frenetic.

Chapter 5

Better public transport, or why buses run around empty

Margaret Thatcher did not do buses any favours. "Any man who takes a bus to work after the age of twenty-six can count himself a failure in life," she declared. Conservative Transport Minister Steven Norris reinforced the point, when he told a committee of MPs in the House of Commons that the problem with public transport was all the unsavoury people you were forced to sit next to. Later on, he said this was not actually his opinion—he loved nothing better than to catch the bus—but that other people said this was why they preferred to drive.

Whether you sympathise with Thatcher and Norris or not, it is sadly true that bus services in many towns and country areas are of a poor quality. The Thatcher Government sold off Britain's municipal bus companies in the middle of the 1980s, supposedly to make things work better by attracting private sector flair and cash, but the sell-off fostered a cheap and nasty industry which cut costs to the bone, and a series of 'bus wars' as rival companies tried to drive each other off the road.

Although some bus companies and some towns are now doing a much better job—and we will hear more about them later in this chapter—there are still many parts of the UK with a rotten bus service. Unfortunately, and perhaps because politicians and the people they talk to travel by bus all too rarely, there is little political pressure to sort out the places where buses are infrequent, unreliable, overpriced and plain dirty. A lot of attention is paid to the railways, but buses are treated as though they are really not at all important. Yet many, many more car trips could potentially be made by bus than will ever be made by train, because buses are well suited for fairly short trips of below 10 miles, which make up about 80 per cent of trips by car. More people use buses than use trains, and they use them more often. Figures from the Government's national travel survey show that, on average, people in Britain travel by bus three times as often as they catch a train. The one exception to this is middle-aged men, who travel by train more often—and this, no doubt, explains why the railways are given more attention by newspaper editors, and in turn why politicians bother about them more.

Listen to some of the things people say about bus services in the rural area where I live. In one village, about 10 miles from Newtown in Powys, I went to a meeting with local people and my friend Nat Taplin to discuss how transport in the local area could be made better. We started by talking about buses, and immediately a slew of problems were raised. The buses were old and often broke down, the bus company did not seem to care, and the services were irregular and infrequent. This was a village on a main road which you might have thought would have a good, regular bus service. What people actually got fell far short of what they might reasonably have expected.

John, an older man who had arthritis which gave him trouble walking, told us: "I think it is lousy, to be honest. I've written a letter to the bus company and told them all we get is reject buses from the inner cities. People like me and another six regular people in Carno can hardly get on them. The 129 bus has no ventilation; the one before that had no heating. I've filled in another questionnaire to the council, contacted the company, and nothing was done. Then I wrote to their head office in Liverpool and look what they sent—a fob-off letter."

The other people in the meeting agreed. One woman, Mary, lived about a mile from the nearest bus stop. She suggested ways the service could be made better: "I'm a keen bus user and I do want to make them viable. Some positive things have happened. We've got a timetable now at the stop which is very useful and we have excellent drivers who will help people with their shopping. But there are frequent breakdowns . . ." (Here, John interrupted to say: "You will get this with reject buses."). Mary carried on: "Modern buses have low steps—to have that would be marvellous. At the moment you can't get a bike on a bus—that would be a good summer thing. They're important for work, college, shopping, but at the moment their times are very inconvenient—if you go to town you either have forty minutes or four hours to go round the shops. In the evening you can get into town but you can't get back. The telephone enquiry number doesn't always answer. There's no Sunday service. We really need real-time information, to know, am I waiting for nothing."

Not all the bus routes in this area are bad. Some villages have a bus into town every hour, and the services run till late in the evening, so you can get back home from the cinema or a concert. But there is a postcode lottery. If you live somewhere where the local council thinks bus services are important, you might get a good service because councils can, if they wish, pay bus companies to run extra buses on unprofitable routes. But cross the border a few miles into another county and the buses may be hopeless.

The same story crops up again and again, especially in rural areas and suburbs of large towns. The bus companies want to make a profit, so they concentrate on the busiest routes. Most of them can make more profit by running a bare-bones bus service than by running a high quality one. It is cheaper to use older buses, not run services in the evenings and at week-ends when the drivers will want to be paid more, and tailor the bus timetable to the number of vehicles they have available rather than the other way round. Many bus companies have a pretty primitive view of marketing and promoting their service, too, despite lots of evidence, which we will look at later, that shows how marketing attracts more passengers.

On top of this, bus companies are allowed to change their timetables at very short notice. They are not obliged to make sure passengers know about the changes, since usually it is the local council that is responsible for putting up timetables at bus stops. One bus company I know of cut its service from one an hour to one every two hours on a main route between two towns, but both the bus company and the council failed to do anything about the timetables at the bus stops, leaving a queue of people waiting by the roadside for over an hour in the days after the change was made.

With so many failings, it is not surprising that many buses run around more than half empty. But could it be different? Stand by the side of the road at 8.30 in the morning and watch the long line of cars, each with one person in it, that pass by within minutes of a near-empty bus, and you cannot help but wonder why it is beyond our collective wit to devise a bus service that those car commuters would use. It is crazily inefficient for fifty people each to drive on their own to roughly the same place at roughly the same time when one driver could get them there.

The answer, unequivocally, is yes, bus services could be transformed so that many car drivers would choose to use them, and the good news is that there are lots of places where this is already happening. The solution is already out there. It is simply a question of copying it. There are three things we should do differently, and this chapter looks at each of them.

First, where people make geographically dispersed journeys, the conventional double-decker bus, or even its smaller sister the hoppa bus, is too inflexible. In rural and some suburban areas, we need to completely rethink public transport. Why can't a bus be more like a taxi?

Second, think of all those people you know who would not be seen dead on the bus, but who happily climb aboard a courtesy hotel-to-airport minibus when they are on holiday. What is the difference? It is to do with image and information—the soft psychological factors again. Get these right and people feel good about catching a bus.

Third, the most profitable bus service is not the same as the best bus service. In this country we have a hands-off approach to buses, with the operators allowed to do whatever makes them the most money, within reason. But some places do it better, and we can learn from them.

* * *

So, why can't a bus be more like a taxi? This might seem an odd question. Buses run to a fixed timetable, on a fixed route, and because no one has to book a bus in advance, it runs whether or not it has any passengers. Taxis, on the other hand, run whenever you want them, wherever you want to go, and they only do a journey if someone books one or hails one in the street. Travelling by taxi is a lot more expensive than catching the bus, so the idea of replacing buses with fleets of taxis does not at first seem at all attractive. In fact, it sounds pretty mad. That is what I thought some years ago when I first heard it. The person who suggested it was an academic, and he and his committee had just completed a report for the Government looking into the future of buses in the countryside. He told me they felt it was hopeless, that there was never going to be a way of running really good bus services in rural areas, and that he had concluded that the answer was to forget about buses and think about taxis instead.

That sounds thoroughly defeatist. Did he mean local councils should pay for taxis for people who were too poor or too old to drive, and that everyone else should be expected to get a car? Well, maybe he did, but there was a grain of truth in what he said, though I did not recognise it till several years later when researching public transport services in Europe. In the late 1990s, in different countries across Europe, a new sort of public transport system started to spring up. It was a cross between a conventional bus and a taxi service, with the advantages of both and the disadvantages of neither. You could book it in advance, like a taxi, but you shared it with other people who were travelling in roughly the same direction at the same time. A few years earlier such services would have been impossible to run, but Global Position Systems-based vehicle tracking and telephone call centre technology had made them viable and affordable.

Lado Weijnands, one of the people responsible for this new type of taxi-cum-bus service in the Dutch town of Maastricht, explained to me how it worked. "When you want to make a journey, you phone a regional call centre. You have to do this at least an hour before you wish to travel. The transport company must pick up each passenger within 15 minutes of their requested departure time. So if you request a taxi for 9.30 p.m., it will arrive between 9.15 and 9.45 p.m. It may have picked up other passengers on the way to your house, or it might make a detour after it has picked you up to collect someone else or to drop them off. The rule is that the total journey must take no more than one and a half times longer than the time it would take you to make the direct trip by car. This gives us the flexibility to combine several trip requests in one journey. Passengers who need to arrive at their destination on time—for example to go to a film or concert—are offered a guaranteed arrival time."

On the buses, twenty-first century style: a modern-day bus controller arranges despatch of a demand-responsive taxibus service after an incoming phone call.

Lado's scheme is one of many that have been set up in different parts of the Netherlands. They grew out of door-to-door taxi services for disabled people, a bit like the community transport schemes that operate in many parts of the UK. On one fairly typical service, in the province of Noord Brabant in the south of the Netherlands, about two-thirds of the passengers were older and disabled people who could not easily use ordinary buses and a third were people who wanted to travel at a time of day when there was no suitable bus. People with a disability had a card that entitled them to pay roughly the same as a normal bus fare, while everyone else paid a premium fare of about twice the bus fare, still quite a lot less than if they had booked an ordinary taxi.

René de Beer, the managing director of another company that provided these taxi-cum-bus services, told me that about half of the cost was met by the local council, with the rest coming from passengers' fares. The taxis and minibuses were driven by local taxi firms, under a contract with a specialist company like René's that co-ordinated the bookings. Taxi firms are used to operating at all hours of the day and night, so there was no problem if a passenger phoned up needing a late night trip. Some of René's services ran 24 hours a day, seven days a week, though this was not always the case. However, long hours were the norm, and even those schemes which were not round the clock usually started for business at seven in the morning and were able to pick people up until 11 o'clock at night.[1]

Imagine a rainbow spectrum of types of public transport service, ranging from a conventional bus at the red end of the rainbow to an ordinary taxi at the violet end, and you would place these door-to-door services at about indigo, close to the taxi end of the spectrum. But there are other options that are more like a conventional bus, which fit in at about yellow on the colour spectrum. One of these is called the Bellbus. This is a service that runs to a regular timetable, like a bus, picking people up at normal bus stops. The difference compared with a conventional bus is that it only runs if at least one person has phoned to book it in advance. The great advantage of the Bellbus is that it can run on quiet routes, and at quiet times of day, when ordinary buses would not be cost-effective. In Friesland, the most northerly province in the Netherlands, some more remote rural areas have a Bellbus service all day, while others have a conventional bus during the day and a pre-book-only Bellbus in the evenings and at weekends. Having to book your trip in advance may not be quite as convenient as simply turning up at the bus stop, but it is a lot better than having no evening bus service at all. Like the door-to-door services that Lado and René were running in the south of the country, Bellbuses have to be booked about an hour beforehand.

The Bellbus is not unique to the Netherlands. In Germany, many areas have a similar service which is known as an Anrufsammeltaxi (it translates roughly as 'call a shared taxi'). Again, the service runs on rural bus routes at quiet times of day when fewer passengers are travelling, but only if a passenger has phoned to request it. For example, a normal bus service might stop in the early evening, but then the Anrufsammeltaxi will take over, running once an hour up till midnight or one o'clock in the morning if someone wants it. This saves the problem of buses running around empty, and it is cheaper for passengers than booking their own taxi. In some places, Anrufsammeltaxi services run throughout the day, and have replaced ordinary buses completely. That might sound like a degradation of the service, but it is a lot better to have an hourly Anrufsammeltaxi that you have to book in advance than a bus that only runs a few times a day. South of the German town of Münster, a shared taxi service called Tax-ibus Lüdinghausen carried nearly 90,000 passengers in 2002, a fourfold increase on the number of people using the old bus service it replaced. More people started using it because the taxibus runs every hour, whereas the former bus service was only two or three times a day.

These new sorts of public transport, a rainbow spectrum of flexible serv-ices that are part bus, part taxi, offer a completely different way of planning transport. They are small-scale solutions writ large: no major infrastructure, but lots of taxibuses spread throughout thousands of communities provid-ing millions of trips a year, at the times people want to travel. The more I found out, the more perfect they seemed. It was not just the Netherlands and Germany that had great examples of taxi-cum-bus services. I came across examples in Denmark and Switzerland, and there are rural areas of the UK with this sort of service too. But while the Dutch, German, Danish and Swiss systems were large-scale and served tens of thousands of passengers every year, most of the British schemes were tiny: one or two vehicles run by pio-neering community groups and some dedicated and valiant volunteers. Because they are small schemes, they cannot achieve the sort of round-the-clock timetables that people like Lado Weijnands and René de Beer were able to offer. In Britain, you would be very lucky to come across a service that operates seven days a week, can get you back from the cinema at half-past ten in the evening, and costs not that much more than the bus fare.

Still, some local councils in Britain are beginning to try the continental approach. It is early days, but there is reason to hope that flexible taxibus services will become common in rural and suburban areas here too. The reason for this optimism is that these types of service are much better value for money than the conventional, frequently empty, bus. In the rural area around Lampeter, the council's public transport co-ordinator Tomi Jones recently let a contract for a daily taxibus, replacing a conventional bus service that used to run around the neighbouring hamlets twice a week. The area is about as rural as they get, with a small and dispersed population. The number of people using the service more than doubled, while the weekly cost of providing the service fell from £600 for two return buses, to £140 for five return taxibuses. As with continental taxibuses, passengers must book their trip to Lampeter in advance, and the service only runs if at least one person has booked it. It is this that reduces the cost. Tomi Jones explained: "The service is being used regularly, but it usually doesn't have to run the whole route. There's nothing running empty now. We've found people are quite happy to book. We try to be as flexible as possible—although we're asking people to book the day before, if someone phones at 8.30 in the morning, we'll do our best to get them on that morning's taxibus." The service to Lampeter is one of five routes that Tomi Jones has switched from conventional bus routes to taxibuses, and he has aspirations to do more. "It takes time to build the ridership," he explained, "but we're getting there slowly, and the money we're saving can be used to put on more services."

If you are lucky enough to live on a main bus route, with buses passing your house every five minutes into the centre of town, you probably will not need a flexible taxibus very often. But for people living in areas that are not so well served, a taxibus service could make the difference between giving up on public transport, buying a car and thenceforward driving everywhere, or being able to pick and mix travel options—taking the bus to work, but booking a taxibus for a night out. Sophisticated call-centre technology and vehicle tracking systems could make it possible to match people and journeys so that there is a bespoke flexible taxi service at almost whatever time you want it. That could make the constant stream of cars, each with one person in it, look like an archaic and crazily inefficient way of organising our transport system. We have only just begun to tap the potential of the taxibus.

* * *

If the first step is designing flexible public transport that fits the journeys people want to make, the second step is an image makeover. You could have the most fantastic bus system in the world, but if everyone thinks it is dirty, shabby and only for society's failures, it will not do well. Nor will it be a runaway success if you need a magnifying glass and a mathematics degree to work out the timetables. It is not enough to make bus services better—you have to grab people and tell them. This would not be news to Orange, Microsoft or Ford, but for bus companies it is a new experience to communicate with their potential customers.

I found out about this in the small town of Aylesbury in Buckinghamshire. Buckinghamshire is a well-heeled sort of county, with more two-car households than almost anywhere else in Britain. It is not very auspicious territory for a scheme to get more people travelling by bus. I went to meet Stefan Dimic, a cheery fellow with a big smile who works for the county council and is responsible for a project they call Travel Choice. At his desk, the phone scarcely stopped ringing and papers were piled high. The floor was an obstacle course of boxes bursting with Travel Choice frisbees, stress balls and post-it pads: freebies to sell the idea that catching the bus is fun.

Three months earlier, Stefan had launched a marketing campaign to boost bus use on a route from Aylesbury town centre to Stoke Mandeville hospital. The council had already gone to a lot of effort to make the buses more reliable on this route. They built a red-tarmacked bus lane. "We called it a red carpet into town," Stefan said. Instead of being held up in a traffic jam every morning and evening, bus passengers got the VIP treatment. Each bus stop had a new timetable and a route map, a new shelter and seats. They put up real-time information screens, so passengers knew when the next bus was due. They even gave the bus stops names. But despite all these improvements, which had cost nearly £3 million for a single bus route, the number of passengers barely changed. Most buses were still poorly used. Few people travelled by bus anyway, so word never got round that the service was better. All this had happened two years ago, and everyone was beginning to wonder if it had been a waste of money.

Stefan and the local bus company chief put their heads together. They decided what was needed was a marketing campaign. The great thing about buses is that they are mobile advertising. The bus company produced a new design, with the words 'every ten minutes' blazed on the back of the bus and a simple diagram of the route on the sides. Stefan commissioned a glossy timetable booklet and brochure. He passed one across to me. "We wanted to make it aspirational to catch the bus," he said. "Look at it—it's meant to look like a Mercedes advert." He was right; I had never before seen such an upmarket timetable. "Then we wrote to everyone who lived within five minutes' walk of the bus route. That was more than 5,000 people. We sent them the brochure and invited them to give the new service a go. We told them they lived within a few steps of the most exciting new transport project in Aylesbury in the last twenty years. We asked them to let us know whether they had tried it and what they thought, and we're about to send out a free one-week ticket to the people who told us they hadn't used it yet."

The effect was electric. The number of passengers jumped nearly a third in a few weeks. Stefan was delighted, but he was not intending to stop there. The day before, he had launched another marketing campaign on a second route. "We intend to continue to promote these services," he told me. "We've started doing days out, parking the buses in the Market Square and handing out balloons. In the past we've made improvements but then rested on our laurels. That didn't work. You've got to keep telling people there's a bus there." [2]

Nearly a year later, I bumped into Stefan again and asked how it was going. Had it been a flash in the pan, with lots of people trying the new bus then giving up and going back to their cars? He grinned. The number of passengers was up 42 per cent and still growing.

Stefan's success story is not an isolated example. Bus companies, local councils and environmental groups have started similar experiments across Britain. In Scotland, the bus company Stagecoach ran a marketing campaign on a route in the town of Perth that they had always thought of as a poor performer. First, they set about improving the service. They put on new low-floor buses, which ran twice as often, and they made the fares easier to understand. The council paid for new shelters and a bus lane to stop buses being held up by traffic. Then Stagecoach began a charm offensive, literally going from door to door to tell people about the improvements. They offered free trips and ran children's competitions and lunches for pensioners. As in Aylesbury, patronage soared, in this case by over 60 per cent. Many of the people who started using the buses were better-off professionals, exactly the people who own more cars and depend on them more.

In Bristol, the council put a lot of money into bus lanes and other improvements on what they called a showcase bus route. They worked with the environmental charity Sustrans to promote the better service, as part of a project called TravelSmart. Sustrans employed community workers who contacted nearly a thousand households to ask if they would like information about green travel options. The information offered was not just about the bus service; it covered walking and cycling as well. There were special bus timetables that were specific to people's own bus journey; a guide to bus services; a cycle map; free one-month public transport tickets to encourage residents to try out the buses; discount cards for equipment from local cycle shops; step-o-meters so people could measure how far they were walking and work out how many calories they were burning. People were offered one-to-one cycle training or a visit by a local bus driver to explain the bus services. The effect? Bus travel went up from an average of 72 to more than 100 bus trips per year for each person. The new bus trips replaced journeys that people had previously made by car.

The special thing about the Bristol project was that Sustrans also measured what happened to a control group of households. These were people who lived close to the showcase bus route and were able to take advantage of the better services, but who were not contacted by the community workers. In the control group, bus travel also rose, but by less than half as much. The extra bus trips replaced walking trips or car passenger trips rather than trips by car drivers, which meant that they had no effect on car mileage.

We have so far focused on buses rather than trains, because buses have so much flexibility and can serve many more destinations. However, marketing and promotion is crucial to train services too. Train companies put substantial effort into marketing their high-speed inter-city train routes, but rather less into the promotion of suburban and regional routes. There is a great deal of untapped potential for attracting drivers out of their cars onto these services. This has been demonstrated in Norfolk, where the train operator, working with the county council and a community rail partnership involving local people, dramatically increased the number of passengers using the line between Norwich and Sheringham. Over the eight years to 2005, journeys on the line almost tripled, from 200,000 to 585,000 per year. Before the work to promote the line started, passenger numbers were declining.[3]

The recipe for success in Norfolk is an interesting one. The involvement of the local community has been important, with local residents and groups becoming involved in improving the appearance and environment around the stations. The line was rechristened the Bittern Line, and promoted to holidaymakers as a way to visit tourist attractions along the route. The community rail partnership organised special events to attract non-users to try the train for the first time, such as live music trains and 'rail ale' trails. This sustained marketing campaign provided the impetus for passenger numbers to grow, and justified investment in more frequent trains and extra late night and Sunday services.

The point about these stories is that if you want to reduce traffic, it is not enough simply to campaign for better public transport. Good bus and train services are a necessary prerequisite to entice people out of cars, but it is also essential to deal with the perceptions that are inside people's heads. Some of the well-heeled citizens of Aylesbury did not know that the bus ran past their front door every ten minutes and could get them to work as quickly as driving, without the hassle of finding a parking space. When Stefan Dimic took the trouble to tell them, they were open-minded enough to try the bus and impressed enough to keep on using it.

Information campaigns will not work if the public transport service really is terrible. If there are no shelters and the only place to wait for the bus is cold and windy, if the vehicles break down and the service routinely runs late, if the trains are filthy and stations are vandalised, those things have to be tackled first. But if the bus or train service is reasonably good, you can persuade a lot more people to use it simply by telling them what is already there.

* * *

So far, we have looked at how to improve buses to suit people's real-life journeys and how to sell the new services so that people try them out. These individual stories are impressive, but on their own they do not amount to much. The trick is to do the same thing across an entire city or country.

You might think that it would be in the interests of public transport companies to provide the best possible service, and that they would be scrambling over each other to do it. But it takes two to tango, and the crucial partner that any bus company needs is a keen local council. Where local councillors are uninterested, the bus company makes more money by running a bargain-basement service, using old buses (the ones that have been replaced by glossy new ones on the showcase routes elsewhere) and stopping early in the evening to save on drivers' overtime wages. By contrast, where local councillors think that public transport is important, they are more likely to bid for government funds for bus lanes, real-time information screens and new shelters for those showcase bus routes. That public investment makes it worthwhile for the bus companies to invest some extra effort too.

It is winner takes all, and incidentally a system that works in favour of larger towns and cities and against rural areas. This is because the only carrot a local council can dangle in front of a bus company is money for capital projects—that is, money for physical changes like bus lanes and smart technology to turn the traffic lights green for buses. In cities, that carrot is attractive because one of the biggest problems bus companies face is that their buses get held up in traffic. This makes services slower, so more buses are needed, and unreliable, so passengers complain. Capital investment helps solve those problems and increases bus companies' profits. In rural areas, capital projects like bus lanes do not make so much difference because traffic is not so congested, so the local councils do not have such attractive carrots to dangle in front of the bus companies' noses.

We will come back to the difficulties in rural areas. First, though, here is an example of a city where the bus company and council are tangoing well: Brighton.

Brighton is the sort of town where you would not be surprised to see a sparkly dressed couple tangoing down the promenade. From the exotic curlicues of the Pavilion, to the besuited businessmen scrunching along the pebbly beach, to the roller-bladers swooshing down the bike lane, there is a sociable, open-minded, try-anything-once feeling about the place. Perhaps that sociability is why people in Brighton seem to like their buses so much, and perhaps it explains how the bus company and the local council have managed to come up with such a successful partnership. Bus trips in Brighton have gone up by 50 per cent in ten years. No other town outside London has done anything like as well; in fact the general pattern elsewhere is that more people are buying cars and bus travel is steadily falling. The popularity of Brighton's buses has helped keep traffic down. With more people choosing to travel by bus, car traffic in and out of the town fell by an eighth between 2000 and 2003.[4]

It is hard to put one's finger on one thing to explain why the buses in Brighton are doing so well, but it seems to be a mixture of some good services and lots of good publicity. As the bus company's chief, Roger French, said: "It is not a physics experiment where one thing is altered at a time. We keep piling in with as many different things as we can think of and it is difficult to step back and say which of those things has contributed how much."

On the main routes, Brighton residents never have to wait more than ten minutes for a bus. Every year, the bus company buys more vehicles and employs more drivers so it can run more services. Wherever you are going, you pay the same fare of £1.20, which is cheap and easy and saves having to find out the fare, then fumble for pennies in the corner of your purse while the other passengers wait. There is no mystery about which bus to catch either: they are colour-coded and there is a metro-style map of the main routes. There is a special express service from housing estates into the city centre which is ideal for commuters—Roger French called it "the motorists' bus" because it suits people who previously drove to work because the buses were too slow.

Brighton Council has done a lot to help too. They built bus lanes and set up a satellite-technology vehicle-tracking system which means they know where all the buses are. This is linked into the computer system that controls the traffic lights, so the lights change to green automatically as a bus arrives. The council is steadily replacing old bus stops with new ones against which low-floor buses can pull right up, so it is easy to get on the bus if you are a mother with a baby buggy or a person who cannot manage steps.

Roger French thinks it is as important to tell people what is being done to make the buses better as it is to do it. This is not just a question of running a publicity campaign when a new service started, or when the flat fare was brought in. "What we've done," he said, "is to create a positive culture which is more than just the metro concept and the flat fare and publicity. It's creating that positive atmosphere. People know that they should be using the bus more. It's all about placing buses in the community, as part of the fabric of the city."

Brighton is exceptional, but it is not unique. Other cities have managed to turn around a historic decline in bus travel too. In Nottingham, bus travel was gently sagging by about 1 per cent a year, but the bus company reversed that by a similar strategy to the one in Brighton—colour-coded buses on each of the main routes out of town, services every ten minutes, buses that keep running till midnight, and lots of publicity. In London, the

'Cheek to cheek': a bus pulls up a few feet from the train at a railway station in North Rhine-Westphalia, Germany. [From a photograph by Paul Salveson]

Mayor, Ken Livingstone, has invested millions of pounds in improving the buses and more Londoners now travel by bus than at any time since the 1960s, when car ownership was far lower. Bus use in the capital city is growing by more than 100 million trips per year, with half of the new journeys being made by Londoners who previously never travelled by bus.[5]

In the countryside, as we have already seen, it is a different story. There is not much co-ordination of services and most bus companies have little incentive to work with the local council. They run services to suit operational convenience rather than what passengers want, and they cherry-pick the most profitable routes and ignore the rest.

It would be far better to do what the Germans, Dutch and Danes do. In those countries, the regional or provincial government decides what public transport is needed and agrees a contract with private bus companies to provide the service. Unlike Britain, where bus companies can be highly selective about which routes they run, this system ensures a comprehensive public transport network. Profitable routes can be used to cross-subsidise less profitable ones. The provincial government sets clear rules for the level of service that should be provided, including how often the buses should run from each village or town, which depends upon its population. For example, in Friesland, all settlements with a population of between 5,000 and 10,000 are guaranteed an hourly service from 7 a.m. until 7 p.m., and a two-hourly service throughout the evening until 11 p.m. Villages with between 250 and 5,000 people have an hourly service at the times people are travelling to and from work, and a bus every two hours during the middle of the day and up to 11 p.m.[6] The services are a mixture of ordinary buses and taxibuses like the Bellbus. The system works: bus travel in rural Friesland is high and growing.

Regional co-ordination also means that the public transport network can be designed so everything—taxibuses, buses and local trains—connects. In North Rhine-Westphalia, a province of Germany, all bus and train services are synchronised. Paul Salveson, an expert on German public transport who also runs the association of community rail partnerships in Britain, described the integration of buses and trains in Germany like this: "It's a cheek-to-cheek system. From the bus exit to the train door is literally a few paces, so transfer is as easy as possible. The buses are timed to feed into and pick up from train services. Through ticketing between buses and trains makes transferring at interchanges that much more straightforward."

The historic neglect of our bus services, and the lack of interest or in some cases absolute disdain felt for them by politicians, are the root causes of the decline in bus travel. However, as we have seen, things could be very different. Demand-responsive services have huge advantages. They can go where you want, when you want, coping with antisocial hours and dispersed populations, and are highly cost-effective. Marketing and promotion can boost the number of people travelling by public transport, and in particular can attract car users who previously never dreamed of getting on a bus. It is perfectly possible to run co-ordinated public transport networks, in which buses are synchronised with trains and the system functions as a seamless whole. Given the right political priority, we could have all of these things, and if we did, many car drivers could be seduced into leaving their car keys at home.

Chapter 6

Cycling without Spandex

Part 1: A trip to Europe

Roland the cameraman is looking worried. He shifts the heavy camera bag on his shoulder and adjusts the sound boom. There are thirty-five of us standing outside a cycle-hire shop in the Dutch town of Utrecht, waiting as the shopkeeper and his assistant wheel out one bike after another and adjust each saddle up or down. They do not seem surprised by so many people wanting bikes at once. I peer into the gloom at the back of the shop: there are plenty more bicycles awaiting hire.

It is 1999, and we are here to find out about the *woonerf*, a Dutch invention which we would like to bring back to the UK. A *woonerf* is a residential street where space has been given back to the residents themselves. Neighbours can socialise in the street and they are safe places for young children to play with their friends. Cars are allowed, but the Dutch law says they must travel at no more than walking pace. The rough translation of *woonerf* into English would be 'living yard', but they have become known in Britain as 'home zones'. Although we have coined this English name for them, as we stand around in the street waiting for our bikes there are no home zones in Britain—they exist only in our imagination.

Graham Smith, the leader of our tour, teaches urban design. Over the years, he has brought hundreds of students to Utrecht to see how the Dutch design their streets. It is a one-person crusade to teach British designers how to do it better. But this is the first time he has brought such a motley group to see the *woonerfen*. We are a mixture of resident-activists who are fighting for the streets we live in back in Britain to be transformed into home zones, professional types from local authorities, a policeman and a civil servant from the Department for Transport. Roland is here to film our fact-finding tour, with Adrian, a film director who is campaigning for his own street in Leeds to be made a home zone.

Graham is adamant that the way to experience Dutch street design is on a bike. He points out the many advantages: you can get from place to place more quickly than if you were walking; you can look around and experience Dutch street life to the full; and the exercise stimulates the brain. Anyway, a coach big enough for 35 people could not manoeuvre into some of the streets we are visiting.

There is only one problem. Roland the cameraman has not ridden a bike since he was nine, and is not at all sure he can remember how. Yesterday we hired bikes in Delft and Roland and Adrian followed in a taxi. But today, Adrian has decided that they missed too much of the action doing this. Graham tends to swerve off the planned route when he sees something interesting, and yesterday the camera missed the best bits.

So Adrian has decided that he and Roland will cycle with us. Roland will have to carry the camera and the sound boom. He will also have to cope with an enormous, heavy sit-up-and-beg bicycle (the Dutch do not go in for mountain bikes) and, worst of all, the bikes we are hiring today have no brakes—or at least, no brakes as we know them; these bikes have a back-pedal brake, which means that if you absent-mindedly back pedal for a moment when cruising downhill, you stop with a shock.

Eventually, we are all fitted with bikes and set off, a straggle of slightly nervous cyclists adjusting to unfamiliar bikes. Several of us are middle-aged, some of the (mostly female) community activists are wearing skirts, though this is no problem because the bikes all have skirt guards. Some of the (mostly male) local authority types are more than a little overweight. In other words, we are an ordinary mix of people, not eager-beaver spandex-clad racing cyclists. Roland does a self-conscious trial run down the cycle lane outside the shop, and manages to stay upright despite an unnerving wobble.

As I look back on this cycling trip around Utrecht, it seems like a dream. In most British cities it would have been a nightmare, but Utrecht is cycling nirvana. There are separate cycle lanes alongside every big road, and when we pulled up at our first major junction we realised there was a phase of the traffic lights especially for us. All the cars from all directions waited as we diagonally crossed six lanes on a marked path, before rejoining a cycle track. Everywhere we went, there were signposts for the cycle routes. In one street, we met two neighbours taking coffee together,

A continental home zone is put to sociable use for an eightieth birthday party.
[Original photograph by Ben Hamilton-Baillie]

sitting at an octagonal picnic table which, with its benches, took up half the width of the narrow street. There was just space for cars to get past. One of the women had lived in the same street for twenty years. She remembered when the authorities first agreed that their street could become a *woonerf*. "They lifted paving bricks outside the houses and told us we could plant flowers. After they had gone, I lifted some more bricks." The street was green with trees and bushes. As we talked, eight children, some only about five years old, cycled past on their way to school. A parent led the way. Each child had a flag on a long pole attached to the bike. Adrian ran after them and asked if they would cycle round the corner again for Roland's film.

Two hours later we turned into another street to see a brightly dressed gaggle of children playing in the town square across the street from their nursery school. The bell rang for the end of playtime and the children walked back across the road. The square had no railings to stop them running into the road. There was a line of bollards to mark the edge of the play space, but that was all. I thought of a school I knew in central London, which had a 20-foot fence separating the playground from the road. Here, there was no need for fences to hem the children in. Cars really did travel along the smaller streets at not much more than a walking pace.

Cycling—or walking—around Utrecht was a joy. The city has its fair share of main roads, but there are separate cycle lanes alongside, so you do not have to be a super-confident speedy cyclist to feel safe. On residential roads, cars travel at 20 miles an hour or less. The Government and the local authorities have spent millions of pounds on traffic calming and *woonerfen*. Lots of the terraced streets have spaces for residents to lock up their bikes. Some have lockable cycle shelters with space for a dozen bicycles.

Cycling is a basic life skill in the Netherlands, something that everyone does. To me, it felt as though cycling and home zones fitted together. On a bike in Utrecht, you could go anywhere and you could cross the city in half an hour, but you were also part of each place you passed through. We could enjoy the atmosphere of the home zones and stop to speak to residents. The people we spoke to felt good about where they lived. One man, Ivar Nijhuis, was outside his house with his two young children, Lucas who was six and Myrthe who was nearly four. "I like living here because it's safe for the children to play," he told us. "There's a little playground at the end of the street where they can go on their own. There are quite a lot of families around here and I know people will look out for them. The people in the street look after the playground together. There's a lot of social cohesion here." Another man said: "Whenever my kid does something he isn't supposed to do, my neighbour comes to my door to tell me. If you want to make a safe environment for your children, it's good for them to grow up in an environment like this." There was a lot of demand for houses in the *woonerfen*. In another street, a resident told us that houses in the *woonerfen* sold quickly. "People buy houses in these areas from estate agents without having even seen them, and we've had fliers through our door asking if we're interested in selling—which, of course, we're not."

Home zones are a physical manifestation of an egalitarian culture which accepts that everyone has a right to use street space—children in go-carts, old people walking slowly with sticks and middle-aged ladies on sit-up-and-beg bikes like the ones we hired, as well as people in cars. It is a culture that respects others and accepts that street space, like any other limited resource, has to be shared; you have to live and let live. Cars are not banned, but motorists are expected to drive in a civilised way. Whereas in the 1970s British town planners were busy designing pedestrian ghettos in town centres and high speed ring roads around them, the Dutch did not try to segregate slow-moving cyclists and pedestrians from fast traffic. Instead, they designed their streets so the different types of traffic could safely mix.

We met the Director of the Dutch Pedestrians Association, Willem Vermeulen, who told us: "Home zones are about so much more than slowing down cars. In Holland, we were lucky. It wasn't hard to encourage other methods of transport as it was not unusual to see chief executives of large corporations hopping onto their bicycles even before we introduced *woonerfen*." He explained that his association was founded in the 1950s because so many children were being killed by car traffic. They campaigned for a 50 kilometres an hour speed limit (30 miles an hour) on residential streets, and got it. But people felt that traffic was still travelling too fast and so the idea of *woonerfen* was born. The first *woonerfen* were implemented in the early 1970s. "Now, we want a maximum speed of 30 kilometres an hour on all residential streets," Willem said. "This lower limit is gradually being extended. But still car traffic is growing."

Even if traffic is still growing, Utrecht feels like a civilised city. People of all ages, fat and thin, teenage girls and company executives, can be seen wearing their everyday clothes and getting around by bike. That, for me, is the key. Cycling in ordinary clothes is a sign of a civilised city. In Utrecht, there is no need to cycle defensively, or to assert your road position, or to cycle at the speed of the traffic, or to wear reflective Spandex or a helmet.

During the 1950s, there was little difference in the number of bikes on the road in Britain and the Netherlands. But while we lost our culture of cycling, the Dutch held on to theirs. The rest of this chapter looks at why we lost our cycling culture in Britain and how we might get it back. But there is a postscript before we leave Utrecht. Six weeks later and back in Britain, I met Adrian to look at the rough cuts of his film. "Guess what," he said, "Roland's bought himself a bike. He says he enjoyed cycling round Utrecht so much that he's going to start cycling here."

* * *

Fifty years ago, millions of people in Britain travelled to work on a bike. Old photographs show hundreds of men on bicycles pouring out of factory gates at clocking-off time. After the Second World War, mileage by bike out-distanced car mileage—Britons collectively cycled about 15 billion miles every year, but only drove about 13 billion miles. But between 1950 and 1970, cycling practically disappeared as a means of transport. By the end of that period, we were collectively cycling about 2 billion miles a year, a fall of over 80 per cent. There was a transformation of our travel habits in the space of less than a generation. Today cycling is so fringe that you are regarded as a near-suicidal freak if you cycle on busy roads, and most bikes on main roads are strapped to the back of 4x4s. But the near-disappearance of cycling as a normal means of travel had largely already happened by 1970; since then, there has been little change. Why did cycling all but disappear here, but not in the Netherlands?

It very nearly happened there too. According to Ton Welleman, a civil servant responsible for Dutch cycling policy, the Dutch have not always been as pro-bike as they are now. In the period up to the Second World War, the Netherlands, like the UK, had many more bicycles than cars. "The Government considered all these bicycles primarily as a source of income," he explained. "A major part of the road plans were financed with the yields of bicycle taxes, which encouraged car traffic." After the Second World War, cycling was still the dominant means of transport, but it was ignored. "Policy makers were primarily occupied with cars and the construction and widening of roads. The bicycle was old-fashioned, a vehicle for the poor. The car symbolised the future, mobility and freedom." [1]

Following almost exactly the same pattern as in Britain, bicycle use in the Netherlands halved during the 1960s. It reached an all-time low in 1972, just before the oil crisis. But then something changed. Ton explained: "Following the oil crises of 1973, many Dutch people rediscovered their bicycles during car-free Sundays." [2] The problems caused by car traffic were also becoming more evident. "The rapidly growing car monster started to bite its own tail," said Ton. "Traffic casualties increased rapidly. Traffic congestion occurred more and more often and the space that parked cars were occupying formed an increasing problem in the cities. Care of the environment was growing, there was more attention paid to healthy exercise, there was an oil crisis . . . and people rediscovered the bicycle as an efficient mode of transport. So a decrease in bicycle use changed into an increase."

Bus shelter with built-in bike parking on a commuting route in Austria:
no soaking saddles here.

Ton Welleman makes it sound easy, almost automatic. But, as we will
see later, the Dutch authorities spent a lot of money retro-fitting city
streets with new layouts that worked for cyclists. They built cycle paths,
redesigned traffic junctions, and built tunnels and bridges especially for
cyclists. They provided neighbourhood storage spaces for bicycles and
made sure that it was easy to park your bike at a train station or take it
on a train. They discovered that cycle parking at bus stops encouraged
people to travel by bike plus bus. And their investment in city street calming, lower speed limits and *woonerfen* created a pleasant environment for
people to cycle.

People often ignore this tremendous effort. Many times, speaking to
city councillors or at public meetings, people have said to me, "But Holland is different. It's flat—not like Sheffield!" or "The Dutch have always
cycled. It's part of their culture," or "It's all very well pointing to what
they do on the Continent, but it rains too much for us to do the same
here." These are all convenient excuses for our past failure, but they do
not stand up to scrutiny. As we shall see later, cycling is a popular means
of transport in mountainous Switzerland as well as the Netherlands; and
it rains as often in bike-mad Copenhagen as it does in Leeds.

The Dutch success story, of turning a decline in bicycle use into growth,
was repeated in Germany. Here again, the bicycle was the most important

means of transport for most people up until about 1950, with more than half of all trips made by bike. But, as American transport planner Heath Maddox explained, "Once automobiles were widely distributed among those who dictated financial and political power in the transportation sector, bicycles were relegated to the fringe, seen primarily as an inferior mode of transportation for the poor working class, women and schoolchildren." [3] By the end of the 1960s, car travel had soared and bike travel accounted for only a twentieth of trips. So great was the indifference—or hostility—to cycling, that cycle paths and tracks built during the 1950s and before the Second World War were dug up to make way for car parking.

Yet, as in the Netherlands, about the time of the 1970s fuel crises, people in Germany started to get on their bikes once more. A combination of high fuel prices, city traffic congestion and growing ecological awareness led to more people choosing to cycle. That heightened awareness and popular demand in turn prompted a concerted programme of bike-lane building, bike-and-rail centres, traffic-calming and cycle parking, so that by the mid-1990s nearly one in eight journeys were made by bicycle, more than double the share in 1970.

The answer to why we in Britain missed out on the cycling renaissance enjoyed by the Dutch and Germans seems to have two parts. First, there were, and are, cultural differences. Environmental awareness came late to Britain, in the late 1980s rather than the 1970s, and by then the problems of petrol shortage from the earlier fuel crises were long forgotten. We did not have the lucky coincidence of social and economic pressures that led people in the Netherlands and Germany to dust down their rusty old bikes, oil the chain, pump up the tyres and rediscover the door-to-door speed and convenience of cycling. That in turn meant that there was little popular pressure on city planners to provide for bicycles. So, instead of building cycle paths, our town planners built dual carriageways. Rather than providing storage for bikes at train stations, we built multi-storey car parks. This is not to say that the Netherlands and Germany escaped the rash of road-building we suffered; far from it. But public pressure meant that the authorities in those countries invested in bike-friendly street design too.

The turnaround in the Netherlands and Germany is impressive. But to understand how it was done and how we could do it in Britain too, I wanted to visit towns and talk to their city planners. I got a chance in winter, 2002. The Department for Transport had set up a group of campaigners and experts to advise it on how to encourage cycling, and it arranged for us to visit three successful continental cities: Freiburg in Germany, Strasbourg in France and Winterthur in Switzerland.

Our trip started in Strasbourg. French towns are not generally cycle-friendly and some are downright hostile to bike around, but Strasbourg is different. In the 1990s, the city spent millions of francs on a new tram system. Building a tram network in an historic city like Strasbourg causes great upheaval: roads must be closed; civil engineering works take many months; there is dust, noise and chaos. But in Strasbourg, the city planners used the opportunity of the building works to renovate squares and streets along the route of the tram. The way they did it makes Strasbourg a delight to explore on foot or on a bike. Arriving in Strasbourg by train, the first you see of this is the grand square in front of the station, Place de la Gare. A road separates Place de la Gare from the rest of the city. Anywhere else, the road would have had the effect of cutting off the coming and going from the station square like a tourniquet around your arm. But here, there was a crossing for pedestrians. Not just any crossing. It stretched along the side of the square, ten, maybe twenty, times wider than normal. I paced it out: it was 50 metres. The traffic lights stopped the cars, and all along the width of the square, people strolled across the road and into the rest of the city. There was no need for the pushing and shoving that happens when a flow of shoppers is corralled into a narrow space. We had all the room we could wish for.

We hired bikes and pedalled off to explore the city. Wherever we went—to the European Parliament, into the city centre, or out into the suburbs—there were cycle paths alongside the roads. Cycling around British cities, paths often stop abruptly where they are most needed. 'Cyclists dismount,' say the signs. Here there were no gaps, and no need to get off our bikes and push. Strasbourg had also cracked another problem that dogs British cities. Here, town planners use guard rails to keep pedestrians apart from cyclists, cars and buses. Guard rails are supposed to make streets safer, but they turn crossing the road into an obstacle course, so pedestrians must either walk three times as far or clamber over the railings. Strasbourg did not use guard rails much. One street had trams running down the centre and a tree-lined boulevard for pedestrians and cyclists alongside the tramlines. Car traffic ran either side of the trams and boulevard and every hundred yards there were junctions where the traffic crossed the boulevard. Any British designer would have received short shrift from the council's chief engineer if they had proposed a street design like this. It would stand no chance of getting off the drawing board. Yet here we were, cycling amid pedestrians, mingling with crossing traffic, able to pull up right by the tram stop, and not a guard rail in sight. It felt like one of the safest, calmest and most civilised streets in a safe and highly civilised city.

On the second day we cycled miles out of the city centre. It was a chilly November morning, but there were plenty of cyclists about. The cycle path came alongside a wide road which our map showed we had to cross, but there seemed no way to reach the cycle track on the other side of the streaming lanes of traffic. We hesitated. Had we lost our way, or had the map misled us into thinking that two sections of cycle route connected when in fact there was an impassable barrier? Then we saw that a cycle subway had been built beneath the road, linking the cycle paths together. Time and again we had similar experiences, in Freiburg and Winterthur as well as Strasbourg, of reaching what seemed an impassable obstacle and finding a cycle path around, above or beneath it. Whereas in Britain cycle paths are often discontinuous, little squiggly worms on a map that do not join up, in these towns all the joining up has been done. The paths connect.

Running out of time before our train, we headed back to the city. We came to a tram stop as a tram pulled up, and stepped aboard with our bikes. No one batted an eyelid. Bikes are not allowed on Strasbourg trams in the morning and evening rush hour, but the rest of the day cyclists are free to hop aboard. Again I was struck by the contrast with Britain, where bikes are banned from trams and restricted on many trains all day long, regardless of how crowded—or empty—the service is.

It is only an hour's train ride across the border from Strasbourg to Freiburg. Get off the train, and one of the first things you notice is a circular building of glass and wood, the city's bicycle station. This bicycle station is popular with commuters. It has space for 1,000 bikes, and you can leave your bike there for the day, or buy a season ticket for a parking space. It has a café and a bike shop, offers bikes for hire, and provides travel information. The building is a tangible demonstration of the high priority that the city gives to bikes.

Freiburg has invested a lot of money and effort in cycling. Martin Haag, one of the city's chief planners, told us promotion of cycling had been central to their policy since the 1960s. "We drew up our first integrated traffic plan in 1969, covering what should be done for trams and bikes. Then in 1971 we drew up the first bicycle network plan. So you see, we've been promoting bicycles for over thirty years. There was another integrated traffic plan in 1979, which gave equal priority to pedestrians, cyclists, public transport and cars. During the 1980s we put a lot of money into our bicycling budget. The peak spending was in 1984, when we spent the equivalent of 3 million euros. That's about eight times as much as we are able to spend now."

The big investment in the 1980s paid for a network of bicycle lanes which run alongside all the main roads in the city and out to the surrounding villages. The length of cycle lane in the city increased from about 18 miles of unconnected bits and pieces, to a dense network of nearly 100 miles of connected cycle lanes. In rural areas outside the city, another 75 miles of bike paths were built.[4] The city also constructed what became known as 'the bicycle highway', a major east-west cycling route right across the city. By 1990, it had become more difficult to find money for building cycle paths, but by then the network was largely complete.

There may be less money for big projects, but Martin and his colleagues are still doing things to make cycling easier and nicer. "Recently we've been changing some streets into what we call bicycle streets," he told us. "Cars are only allowed in for access, and cyclists can use the whole width of the road. The speed limit is 15 kilometres an hour, though actually some of the cyclists go a bit faster than that." Although there are only short lengths of bicycle street spread around the city, they are used by about 10,000 cyclists every day.

One of the planners' headaches is how to provide enough parking space for bicycles. "We've got cycle parking spread throughout the city centre," said Martin. "Fifty spaces here, twenty spaces here, nine spaces there. It adds up to more than 5,000 spaces altogether. Some of the cycle parking is in areas that used to provide parking for cars. There's an area in front of the university which used to provide forty car parking spaces, and now it can park up to 400 bikes. We've also put in bike parking next to the tram stops, with roofs so the bikes stay dry."

Freiburg stuck at it when it came to cycle promotion. For thirty years, it steadily built new cycle lanes, provided short-cuts for cyclists, and ensured there were plenty of cycle stands where its citizens could lock up their bikes to go shopping, run an errand or catch the tram. The effort was worthwhile. In the last twenty years, Freiburg's citizens have made more and more trips by bike, and progressively fewer by car. Martin Haag told me that in 1982, roughly one in seven of the average Freiburger's daily trips were made by bike (15 per cent). By 1999, the figure was more than one in four (26 per cent).

This is not a city obsessed by bikes to the exclusion of all other transport. Travel by public transport has also grown. This is partly because the city's population has risen: more inhabitants mean more public transport trips. But if you strip out the effect of population growth and look at how often each person gets on a bus or tram, it is clear that each individual is travelling more now by public transport than twenty years ago. The average Freiburg resident made about one trip in ten (11 per cent) by public transport in 1982. By 1999, nearly one in five (18 per cent) of the average resident's trips were by public transport. The surge in bus and tram travel happened because the city's publicly owned transport company brought in a season ticket which could be used by friends and family as well as the holder.[5] It was called an Umweltschutzkarte, or environmental protection ticket, and its transferability and low price (the new monthly season ticket was three-quarters the price of the ticket it replaced, and the cost stayed the same for over six years) encouraged regular travel by bus and tram. In the year after the new ticket was brought in, about 3,000-4,000 regular car drivers switched to using public transport.

There is another side to the Freiburg story. Alongside the initiatives to make travel by bike and public transport more attractive, the city planners were determined to keep cars under control. "The measures to reduce car use focused on the city centre at first," Martin explained. "The shopping area was closed to traffic in the 1970s, although we still allow residents to drive their cars in the centre in the evening because we want to encourage people to live in the centre of town. Then in the mid-1980s we brought in a speed limit of 30 kilometres an hour on all residential roads. There are parking charges in the city centre and in local shopping centres."

Freiburg's residents cycle and catch the bus a lot, but they also own and use cars and, as elsewhere, car ownership is growing. However, the average distance each Freiburg family travels by car is going down. More people own cars, but they now use them less than in the 1980s. The change in travel patterns was gradual over several decades. There was no quick fix. The lesson from Freiburg is that with sustained effort and investment in public transport and bike networks, it is possible to reverse the trend towards ever greater dependency on cars.

We left Freiburg for the final stop of the tour, Winterthur in Switzerland. Winterthur is a small prosperous town of 90,000 inhabitants which nestles in a valley between seven hills. Herbert Ernst of the town's traffic department met us at the station and took us down the platform to hire bikes from the station's cycle centre. It was a smaller affair than the round bicycle station in Freiburg, but had plenty of bikes for hire. Bike hire for the day cost just a few francs, a fraction of the cost in Britain. As in Freiburg, the cycle centre provided parking for train commuters and cycle repair services. Commuters who work in Zürich can cycle to the station in the morning, leave their bikes to be serviced and pick them up in the evening.

We set off on a tour of the town, with Herbert Ernst leading the way. The first stop was a derelict site with old warehouses near the station, the site of a planned development which when finished would house 15,000 residents, offices and workplaces. "This will be a major development," Herbert explained. "But although a lot of people will be living here, we'll only have parking space for 1,500 cars, one parking space for every ten inhabitants. Most of the development will have pedestrian and cycle access only, no cars." The scheme epitomised the best principles of sustainable land use planning: located close to the railway station and with bus services running nearby; safe easy access for pedestrians and cyclists; and limited parking which would discourage future occupiers from running a car.

Still, the map of Winterthur did not suggest a promising location for cycling. The town centre is flat but hemmed in by steep wooded hills. A busy road runs along each of the six valleys that radiate from the town. Many people live in the villages along these valleys. It reminded me of the area of Wales where I live: small towns nestling between hills, with main roads through the valleys and the few remaining cyclists forced either to brave the high-speed traffic or to push up one-in-six hills on the minor lanes. The difference in Winterthur was that the main roads in the valleys all had a cycle path alongside, so residents of the surrounding suburbs and villages could safely and comfortably cycle into the town centre. It ought to be obvious— cyclists need as flat a route as possible, and if there are too many steep inclines, most people will be put off cycling and will drive instead.

In Britain, local council transport planners often claim that it is too difficult to put in cycle routes. "It's different in Europe," they say, "the roads are wider, there's more space and fewer obstacles." But it was clear in Winterthur that the town planners had faced many practical difficulties too. The planning of the cycle routes was a pragmatic affair. One of Herbert's colleagues, Guido Brunner, later explained. "We don't have any general rules for the cycle routes. It's a question of the local place, the speed limit, the intensity of the traffic and so on. The circumstances are more important than any concept of optimal routes."

In all, the town has over 100 miles of dedicated cycle lanes and tracks. Herbert showed us a series of maps of how the cycle network had grown. It started slowly. The first step, in the 1950s, was to close about five miles of minor roads to cars, parallel to the main arterial roads through the valleys. The minor roads were reserved for cyclists. By 1970, a few cycle paths had been built, and the total length of dedicated cycle routes had risen to about eight miles. Then things took off. By 1980, the cycle route map started to look like a proper network, not just a few wiggly, disconnected lines, and the length of cycle paths had risen to 25 miles. By 1990, it had reached 50 miles, and by 2000 it had topped 100 miles.

The town's planners realised that each route was only as good as its weakest link, and that it was vital to close gaps where a route was obstructed by a busy road or severed by a railway line. During the 1980s they built seven underpasses to close gaps in the network. These were costly. Herbert took us to see a cycle and pedestrian subway which had recently been built under the main railway line, saving a long detour to the nearest road bridge. "Yes, it was an expensive and difficult project," he told us, "but worth it because we believe that cycling is important." Herbert was already planning another cycle subway beneath the railway, close to the town's main railway station.

As in Freiburg, residential roads in Winterthur have a speed limit of 30 kilometres an hour, or a bit less than 20 miles an hour. Cyclists are allowed to cycle the 'wrong' way down one-way streets, which makes it easier to take a direct route to your destination. Traffic planners in Britain might raise an eyebrow at this dangerous practice, but the statistics show that cycling in Winterthur is safe. Despite the many cyclists, and the growth of car traffic, cyclists are involved in a third fewer crashes now than thirty years ago.

The high priority given to cycling by Herbert and his colleagues is unusual, and Winterthur has a reputation within Switzerland as 'a cyclists' city'. About a quarter of the town's population commute to work by bike and over a third of schoolchildren and students cycle to school or college. As in Freiburg, Herbert Ernst emphasised that this was the result of vigorous effort and substantial investment over a long period. "How have you

Everyday cycling in Langenlois market, Austria, and not a shred of Spandex in sight.

done it?" I asked him. "We started early," he explained, "and we've been promoting cycling for the last 20 years."

As we cycled around Winterthur, I was struck by the ordinary dress of the people we saw on their bikes. There was not much sign of cycle helmets or reflective jackets or shiny leggings. Looking through the photographs of cycle tracks that Guido Brunner emailed to me a few months later, I can count three cyclists wearing helmets, three sporty-looking men in Spandex cycle shorts, and forty-three ordinary-looking men and women in their everyday clothes, most riding upright bikes. There are few drop-handlebar racing bikes or hybrids. Few of the people in the photos seem even to bother with cycle panniers. They have handbags slung into wicker baskets or briefcases strapped onto racks, or shopping bags dangling from the handlebars. The photographs are eloquent: by their dress the residents of Winterthur are showing that in their town, you do not need to worry about special cycling clothes because there is no need to get sweaty keeping up with the speed of the traffic. You can cycle as slowly or as fast as you like. There is no need to wear a reflective jacket, because you are safe from the cars anyway. You do not even need to worry too much about how to carry the shopping—if it is in a carrier bag hanging from the handlebars and it swings into your front wheel, the worst that is likely to happen is that you may fall off and graze a knee. There will be no more serious consequences. Cycling in Winterthur is an ordinary everyday activity.

I left Winterthur feeling puzzled about how the lessons of that town, and Freiburg and Strasbourg, could be applied in Britain. We had seen that it takes a long time to make a city cycle-friendly, and you have to stick at it for twenty years or longer. Freiburg and Winterthur had been plugging away since the 1970s, although Strasbourg had achieved a lot in a shorter time. Most British cities are at least twenty years behind, and it will take some time for them to build the sort of cycle infrastructure that the cities we visited now enjoy.

In all three towns, we had noticed the continuity of cycle routes. In Britain there are so many places where cycle paths disappear just when the traffic conditions get difficult. You almost never hear of a local council spending a large sum on a difficult engineering project like the cycle subway beneath the railway line in Winterthur, because no one really believes that it is worth spending lots of money on cycling. The politicians and planners in the towns we visited evidently felt that cycling was important, and worth investing in, even to the extent of tackling quite challenging problems with costly civil engineering.

Strasbourg, Freiburg and Winterthur had all built extensive networks of connecting cycle routes, but they had done a lot more besides that. In all three towns, speeds in residential roads were limited to less than 20 miles an hour. Strasbourg had designed fine public squares, streets and boulevards that were a delight to walk in or cycle through and they had built a fine new tram system. In Winterthur, we had seen how large housing developments should be planned so that their future residents can travel by public transport, foot and bike.

The high priority attached to cycling had resulted in large budgets. In Freiburg, over the period of ten years during which most of the cycle network had been built, the city spent 1-2 million euros per year and at the peak spent over 3 million euros in one year. That is equivalent to spending between £4 and £10 per inhabitant, every year for a decade. In contrast, British towns each year spend an average of £1 per inhabitant on cycle facilities. In some towns the figure is pitifully low. I asked the Department for Transport in Britain how much money each local council reported spending on cycling schemes in the last five years. The results did not make encouraging reading: Leeds, 74 pence per inhabitant per year; Stockport, 34 pence; Portsmouth, 20 pence; Bolton, 15 pence. It took

Freiburg many years to build its cycle network, but at the rate some British towns are investing it would take a century.

The question puzzling us was how to persuade politicians in Britain to back large-scale investment in cycling, in towns where few people now ride a bike. It was one thing for the politicians in Freiburg to embark on an ambitious programme of cycle lane building, knowing that many of their citizens (and voters) already cycled. But in cities with little culture of cycling, politicians base their decisions on the view through the car windscreen, because that is all they know, and there is little pressure from family, neighbours, friends, the local newspaper, local businesspeople or all the others they have contact with, to do anything differently. The catch is that where few people cycle, little will be done to make cycling more attractive. It is a difficult task: to rebuild a culture of cycling in the absence of good conditions, so that politicians are spurred to invest in facilities to encourage more people to cycle, more often.

With so many difficulties, is it worth the effort? I firmly believe that it is. Much of the car traffic in and around towns is caused by people making short trips that would be as quick by bike. There is so much potential for these trips, up to about five miles, to be cycled, and if they were, our towns and villages would be quieter, cleaner and safer. The bicycle fills a gap in the spectrum of green travel options between walking and catching the bus, and without it it is hard to imagine a truly sustainable city.

Part 2: Back in Britain
Britain missed out on the flowering of cycling and reclaiming of city street space that took place in the Netherlands and Germany during the 1970s, but it could still happen here. One person who is trying to bring it about is John Grimshaw, founder of the cycle-path and sustainable transport charity Sustrans.

John is an unlikely cycling advocate. He trained as a civil engineer, and many of his contemporaries went on to make a comfortable living from building new bridges and motorways. He is tall and magisterial, almost invariably tweed-jacketed, with a well-to-do accent. In another life he might have been the headmaster of a prestigious public school. But in fact, he has dedicated most of his working life to building cycle paths. Starting from small beginnings, the result is the National Cycle Network, built by Sustrans in partnership with hundreds of local authorities, local cycling groups and other partners. By 2005, there were some 10,000 miles of national routes, across England, Wales, Scotland and Northern Ireland. Every year, they carry well over 120 million trips, roughly two-thirds cyclists and one-third pedestrians, and their use is increasing fast, with 10 per cent more cyclists on every mile of route every year.

It all started in the 1970s. John Grimshaw was a member of a Bristol-based cycling group, Cyclebag, trying to get the council to listen but making little headway. "The campaigning group was frustrated at the difficulty of making any political progress," explained John, "so we said we would do it ourselves." They formed a trading company to buy stone, and started building a cycle path along a disused rail line between Bristol and Bath. "We built the first eight kilometres and it was immensely successful. Those of us who were doing it said, right, it's quite clear that every town in the country needs one of these, as a place to learn to cycle again. So our first ambition was that every town should have a good long path. We started in the West Country: in Plymouth, where we leased land from China Clays, in Swindon, Cheddar, Cheltenham. Basically we did places round about."

That first cycle path, the Bristol and Bath Railway Path, now carries 1.5 million cycle trips per year, yet before it was built almost nobody would have cycled along any part of that route. People use it to cycle to work, to school, or for a weekend afternoon out. Sustrans has sometimes been criticised for building off-road routes that are mainly used for leisure trips, but John points out that many of its traffic-free paths are heavily used by commuters, schoolchildren and shoppers. Still, he is unrepentant about providing an attractive place for leisure cycling: "I've always seen it as critical to have a positive strategy to start people cycling again—and you don't start with the journey to work. The way into cycling, that first journey, will almost certainly be a leisure journey. Other northern European countries have achieved much higher levels of cycling. It's obvious that we should as far as possible replicate what they have been doing, and that means huge numbers of high quality routes."

With some successful paths in the south-west under their belts, John and his colleagues were itching to look further afield. "The next move was that the Government Minister for Transport at the time, in 1981, was invited to come and see the path on a Sunday. He came down with his wife and kids, and we absolutely flooded the path with cyclists. The only problem was, of course, everyone asked him, are you the minister?" Still, the minister was impressed. "So, the result was that he commissioned us to do a study of railway path opportunities in England and Wales. I knew right from the start that nothing would happen with it, so we persuaded them to fund us to do thirty-three appendices. Every appendix was about a possible cycle path in a different county, and I wrote them all with the intention that we would build them. So that was the foundation for the next few years' work."

During the 1980s, Sustrans benefited from Government unemployment schemes, which provided a large workforce of helpers to build cycle paths. It also relied heavily on volunteers, and sometimes on imaginative ways of obtaining raw materials. In 1985, the cycle campaign group in Edinburgh, Spokes, invited John to a meeting to speak to the city council. John explained what happened: "The immediate decision we took was that that summer we would build a path in Edinburgh on a voluntary basis. We built the path in one week with about sixty volunteers. I sent a couple of guys off to filch some huge timbers I had spotted and as they were acquiring these massive timbers the police turned up and wanted to know what was going on. It turned out that one of the volunteers was a top civil servant in the Scottish Office. He flashed his pass at the policemen, and they said, 'Oh, that's all right, sir, just carry on.'" The work in Edinburgh led to a study of all the former rail lines in Scotland and it also resulted in the Scottish Office paying for a Loch Lomond demonstration project.

By the early 1990s, Sustrans had worked in England, Wales and Scotland and was well established as a national organisation. But the really big break came with a bid to the National Lottery Millennium Commission. "We were only able to do the millennium project because we had fifteen years preparing for it," explained John. "We put the bid in without Northern Ireland and we were hauled in by the lottery director who said we like your bid but you've got to include Northern Ireland. So we phoned our five or so supporters there and said we've got to have a scheme by Monday morning. And that's how Northern Ireland came into it." The Millennium Commission contributed £43.5 million towards the cost of building 5,000 miles of national cycle network by 2000.

The National Cycle Network is not the be-all-and-end-all of cycle route building. In fact, it is just a beginning. But it is symbolically important, and John believes its existence has persuaded many local authorities to give a higher priority to cycling. "In the early days we were using the network to try and make progress where there really was no support for cycling. So we would say to a local council, look, we were thinking of bringing the national network through your town, but it depends on you doing something too. It was always seen as a way of swinging around councils that did nothing, to get them to do something for cycling. Secondly, we were interested in trying to raise the status of cycling. Perhaps it's too subtle an idea, but we were saying, look, if it's worth us building a national network for cycling, it's important enough for you to do something too."

Work by John Grimshaw, and others like him, has inspired many British towns and cities to invest in cycling. But what can be done if the local authority in your area sees cycle-lane building as bottom of its priorities? What do you do if your town spends a fraction of what is needed on cycling? I think part of the answer is that it is necessary to identify the fertile areas where it might be possible to build a cycling culture from the bottom up—where the geography, traffic conditions and social situation are right. In these places, action by campaigning groups and individuals can get more people cycling, and this in turn may prompt politicians to act.

This is what happened in London, an unlikely place for a cycling renaissance but nevertheless the city where cycling is now growing faster than anywhere else in Britain.

In the 1980s, I lived in the inner London borough of Hackney. It is one of the poorest London boroughs, and suffers from terrible traffic noise and pollution. It also had poor public transport; it was the only London borough without a tube station, and buses were notoriously unreliable because the roads were chock-a-block with cars and lorries. Hackney was not blessed with good conditions to encourage cycling. There were a few cycle lanes but they were often filled with broken glass or rubbish, and cycle theft and vandalism were common. At the beginning of the decade, few people in Hackney cycled regularly. But through the 1980s and 1990s, ever so slowly, more people started to do so. Between 1981 and 2001, the number of people travelling to work by bike climbed by several thousand. The numbers were still tiny, but cycling in Hackney was on the rise. Over twenty years, the dry figures from the national census show that cycling in Hackney almost tripled: that is, in 1981, just 2.5 per cent of Hackney residents cycled to work, but by 1991 this had climbed to 4 per cent and by 2001 it was nearly 7 per cent.

No one would have guessed that Hackney would emerge as the place where cycling would grow fastest. The council had a reputation for being inefficient and crisis-ridden; there were enormous problems of poverty, crime and poor housing, which meant little money was available for traffic calming or cycle lanes; and few officers stayed in the council's transport department long. Hackney's bicycle renaissance did not happen because a benevolent local authority created an environment conducive to cycling.

The trend in other inner London boroughs was similar. John Parkin analysed the shifting fortunes of cycling in all 376 districts and boroughs in England and Wales, as revealed by the national census. Although Hackney topped the list of places where cycling increased between the 1981 and 2001 censuses, other London boroughs also did well. Of the top ten councils nationwide, five were from inner London: Hackney, Islington, Hammersmith and Fulham, Lambeth and Camden.[6]

This raises an intriguing question. More people started cycling in inner London during the 1980s and 1990s in spite of the traffic, the lack of cycle lanes, the lack of cycle parking stands (and the exasperating attitude of the police that if you locked a bike to a railing in central London it should be destroyed because you might be a terrorist and the bike might have Semtex explosive packed into its frame). Little was done to improve London's streets during this twenty year time-span. So why did more people start cycling? Partly, I think it was because the alternatives were so unattractive. Cycling was one of the quickest ways to get around, beating the bus or car because cyclists could nip through the jams. In Hackney, part of the explanation might also have been that the borough had a long history of radicalism, and started to attract young people who were environmentally aware and predisposed to cycling. In other words, the underlying conditions were favourable.

But I also believe that cycle activists played an important part in that cultural shift. For years, volunteer campaigners associated with the London Cycling Campaign provided practical help to get people cycling. They researched good cycling routes and published maps, ran Dr Bike surgeries to help novice cyclists repair punctures and replace brake cables, offered bike 'buddies' to help people become confident on two wheels and find good routes to work or college. They ran community cycling projects, reaching outside the clique of middle-class greenies to people who had never considered that cycling might be for them. They had a lot of fun, with Sunday social rides and bike festivals.

All this work helped shape attitudes to cycling inside people's heads. Changing attitudes so that more people start cycling on the routes where they can is a crucial step. It can deal with the subjective reasons for not cycling: lack of confidence; not knowing that there is a good, quiet back road route; worrying about what will happen if you get a puncture. It is also a 'selling' exercise, a process of convincing people that a bike fits with their lifestyle—that it is fun, or healthy, or quick, or cheap, or practical, or flexible, or all of those.

In 2000, Londoners for the first time elected a mayor to run the whole city. They voted in Ken Livingstone, who promised to make it his top priority to sort out London's creaking transport system and who announced that he would chair Transport for London (TfL), the new organisation set up to run public transport and manage London's main roads. Livingstone and TfL did several things that gave cycling a boost. The most dramatic was the central London congestion charge of £5 which drivers had to pay every day they used a car in an area of about 8 square miles at the heart of the city. The charge was introduced in school half-term week in February 2003. The choice of half-term week was deliberate: no one, anywhere in the world, had run a scheme like this before, and no one really knew what would happen. There was a risk that drivers would stay in their cars, but divert around the congestion charging zone to avoid paying, causing a traffic surge on the surrounding road network. If that happened, the lighter traffic in half-term week, with no school run and many families taking a short holiday, might be just enough to avert gridlock, and could be the difference between the scheme being hailed as a success or slated as a disaster.

The congestion charge had an immediate and dramatic effect. Journalists and motoring organisations had been predicting chaos, but in the event there was no traffic surge on the roads around the central charging zone. Traffic entering central London fell decisively by 14 per cent on the first day, and stayed at that level in the months that followed. The difference was roughly equal to that between weekday and weekend traffic, and was immediately obvious to anyone walking, driving or cycling within the zone. Traffic flowed more smoothly and the streets felt safer and calmer.

People adapted to the congestion charge in various ways. The dominant effect was that drivers switched to the bus or tube. However, the fall in traffic also encouraged many former car drivers to cycle, and as a result of this the number of cyclists on roads leading into the central zone went up by a fifth. Six months after the charge had been brought in, TfL carried out a survey of Londoners' travel habits, and found that residents of inner and central London were using a bike more often for their trips into the city centre.

The second thing TfL did was to boost the money available for cycle schemes. By 2004, its budget allowed £12 million for cycle lanes and cycle parking, equivalent to about £1.50 per London resident, and the following year the budget was £17 million, or £2.20 per resident. This was less than in Freiburg, but it was a beginning, and quickly showed results. As each stretch of cycle lane was installed, the number of cyclists using that route went up. More than half the cyclists on one new cycle track along Cable Street in inner east London said that the improvements had persuaded them to cycle more in the area.

Working with the London Cycling Campaign, TfL published a series of maps of cycle routes. Nineteen maps were needed to cover the whole city. The campaign group had been mapping good cycling routes across the capital for many years, but the partnership with TfL meant the guides could be given out free. More than 2 million were distributed. In a city as large as London, people do not necessarily know whether there will be a good cycling route for a particular journey, so the maps were almost as important as the routes themselves. When TfL spoke to users of the maps, a quarter of the people they interviewed said that they were beginner or occasional cyclists, and almost all were enthusiastic about how the maps had helped them. Half of all the map users said that they were now cycling more often.

It is difficult to measure the overall effect of the congestion charge, the new cycle tracks, the guides, and so on. As we have seen, cycling in inner London was going up anyway. Nobody could say for certain that the TfL schemes were the cause of any measured increase. A further complication was that people cycle less or more according to the weather and the time of year. A graph of cycling levels is never a straight line. It looks like the rounded bumps of the Loch Ness monster, lows marking the winter and highs corresponding to the summer.

Nevertheless, looking at the graphs of what is happening in London, I feel excited. Hidden in pages of dense committee reports, the graphs record the amount of cycling every month on London's main roads. Each year the winter-time hollows and the summer-time bumps are higher up the chart. In European cities like Strasbourg and Freiburg, cycling grew by about 5 per cent a year. But these bumps and hollows suggest that growth in London is faster—10, maybe even 20 per cent a year. Against all the odds, cycling in London is experiencing a boom.

London's cycling success is surely partly the result of better cycle lanes, but it also reflects a cultural shift. Ken Livingstone and his transport planners in TfL are now responding to the surge in demand, but it is nice to think that they are doing it because of the determination of ordinary Londoners who gave their spare time to building that groundswell of demand in the first place.

Part 3: Selling cycling

The story of London gives hope that it is possible to re-create a culture of cycling in Britain. It will take time—perhaps twenty years—but we know from European towns that steady year-by-year investment and support for cycling can effect great change. The important thing is to start now, and to keep on going.

However, there is one more lesson we need to take to heart, this time from Denmark. This lesson is that building bike lanes alone may not necessarily persuade drivers to switch from four wheels to two. A good safe bike route is a necessary prerequisite for someone to cycle, but they must also be persuaded to give cycling a go. Once again, the soft psychological techniques are as important as the small-scale physical changes to the street environment. To make sure bike lanes are well used, we must sell cycling.

If you are trying to sell something to someone, it is important to have a good idea of what might persuade them to buy it. Marketing persuades us to buy things based on image, branding, the picture on the front of the packet, and the values associated with it. The process of selling cycling to people who have never thought of getting on a bike is more complex and subtle than selling, say, soap powder, but the research techniques that marketing experts use can help us understand how to persuade people to give cycling a go. For example, is it more effective to emphasise that cycling is green, or that it is cheap, or that it is a good way of getting exercise?

One finding that crops up repeatedly is that health benefits are a strong motivation for people to cycle more often. Once they get started, they discover that a regular half-hour cycle ride to work or the shops makes them feel more energetic, and within a month or two a few pounds of flab round the tummy have mysteriously disappeared. For some people, cost is important, and in some areas the hassle associated with driving is also significant. A survey by TfL found that the reasons people gave most often for increasing their cycling were 'cycling is healthy' (three-quarters of the people interviewed mentioned this reason); 'cycling is cheaper than the alternatives' (two-thirds said this); and 'the roads are too congested when driving a car' (nearly two-thirds said this).[7] Similar results came from a national survey, this time of people who had decided to cut back on using the car for short trips, and to walk or cycle instead. The strongest motivation for people to change their travel patterns was that they wanted to get more exercise (mentioned by a third of those surveyed), whereas only 8 per cent were walking or cycling more because they wanted to help the environment.[8] The lesson is clear: if you want to persuade someone to cycle, don't say it's green. Say it will make them fit and healthy. Personal benefits are more motivating than abstract benefits to the wider community.

As well as giving people reasons for cycling, it is important to deal with the obstacles that prevent people getting on their bikes. Although fear of traffic and lack of decent cycle lanes are major obstacles, they are not the only ones. The TfL survey asked about a long list of possible barriers that, if removed, might persuade people to try cycling. About a third of people who never cycled said that they might change their minds if various problems were tackled. As expected, providing more cycle lanes figured high on people's wish-lists. But 'someone else doing the bike repairs' was even more important. 'Having secure cycle parking at work' and 'training on cycling in London' were also high up.

These surveys are intriguing. Might they point to another way of getting people out of their cars and onto two wheels? The town of Aarhus in Denmark was the location for an experiment to find out. It was called BikeBuster.[9]

Aarhus is the second largest city in Denmark, about the size of Nottingham, with some 100,000 people commuting into the city centre every day. The BikeBuster project set out to persuade motorists to choose the bike instead of the car for their trip to work. BikeBusters caught the imagination of many ordinary Aarhusians, and about 1,700 of them volunteered to take part. This was many more than the project could cope with, and after a rigorous weeding process the project organisers chose 173 people, all daily car travellers who lived in the suburbs up to five miles from the town centre, representing a balanced mix of ages, sex, and geographic location.

The 173 people—nicknamed the BikeBusters—were offered a new bicycle of their own choice, fitted with a child seat (if they wanted), a carrier, bike lights, a lock, and a bicycle mileometer. They were given good quality raingear, an umbrella and gloves and they could have the bike repaired or serviced as often as necessary, for free. There was a free one-year season ticket for public transport and bus service timetables, useful for days when it was too cold, snowy or rainy to cycle. The BikeBusters were also offered a free health check, to find out what effect cycling was having on their weight, fitness and blood pressure. There was a newsletter to keep them informed about the project and encourage them to stay involved.

In return, the BikeBusters promised to leave the car at home as much as possible, and to contribute to the project by filling in questionnaires and trip diaries. Although they all made this promise, in practice there was nothing apart from moral pressure to force anyone to change their travel behaviour. The report of the project shows that its organisers were not completely confident of what would happen, especially when winter arrived:

"As all the participants . . . were strongly motivated and had entered into a 'contract'. . . about putting their back into it, it was expected that the summer period would give a considerable transfer from car to bicycle, while it was a little more uncertain that inveterate motorists would stand up to wind and weather and continue to cycle in the winter period."

The project started in February, with a survey of the BikeBusters travel habits before they took delivery of their new bikes. From Monday to Friday during a week in February, each BikeBuster made about sixteen trips by car, plus two bike trips and two trips on foot. Their level of car use was almost identical to that among car drivers in Britain, despite the image we have of the Danes as cycling a lot and being ecologically minded. These people were, as the project researchers described them, 'inveterate motorists'.

Through the spring and summer, the BikeBusters started cycling, and by September a second travel survey showed that each of them was typically making about six car trips per week, ten bike trips, two trips on foot and one trip by bus. So far, so good: car travel had more than halved, and cycling had soared. The acid test, though, would be the winter months. Once the weather became cold and rainy, the BikeBusters might slip back into driving to work, or drop out of the project altogether. You can imagine the project researchers sending out the winter travel survey in some trepidation about what results they might get back.

They need not have worried. Of the original 173 BikeBusters, 23 had by now officially dropped out or did not return the survey, but 150 people were still sufficiently keen to return the form. From Monday to Friday during a week in March, each BikeBuster made just over seven car trips— slightly more than during the summer, but not much. They made five trips by bike, three on foot, and three by bus. Reading the reports of the researchers, you can sense that they felt pleased: "The BikeBusters stick to the good cycling habits. The good health, the good bicycle clothes and gloves, have made it possible to cycle all through the year."

The project officially finished at this point. The BikeBusters were offered the chance to buy the bikes they had been using for the last twelve months at a bargain price. The researchers record that a few of the families had started off with two cars, but decided that they could meet their travel needs with just one car plus a bike, and sold the second car. With this sort of project, though, there is always the question, what happened afterwards? What happened once the BikeBusters stopped getting free bike maintenance and encouraging newsletters? So, six months later, the researchers sent out one more travel survey. They found that the BikeBusters' travel patterns had remained almost exactly the same. Once having got into the habit of cycling, they were still on their bikes, and using their cars dramatically less.

The BikeBusters project is important for several reasons. First, it highlights that even in a country like Denmark, which has a strong culture of cycling and an excellent network of cycle paths, people use their cars thoughtlessly, for trips where a bike or the bus would do the job just as well. The Danish 'inveterate motorists' were able to more than halve the number of trips they made by car. The evidence from Aarhus suggests that, even where adequate cycle routes already exist, there is work to be done to persuade people to use them instead of grabbing the car keys. Second, the project showed that many habitual car users are interested and willing to cut their car use, and that if offered encouragement and a helping hand they can make large changes to their travel patterns. Of course, not all car users are interested and willing, but that does not, for the moment, matter. The point is to start by offering help to those people who do want to change their lifestyle. If more of them start cycling, others will eventually follow.

I would like to see hundreds of projects like BikeBusters, in every town in Britain, offering practical help to interested people living in areas with reasonably good cycle routes. My ideal package would be tailored to local circumstances, but could include:

- the loan of a good bike to people who did not own one, or free servicing of their old bike to make it roadworthy

- free bike maintenance provided by a local cycle shop, with users able to drop off their bikes for servicing at convenient collection points: at work, at school or at a nearby supermarket

- free cycle training, covering basic skills for beginners and advanced skills, including coping with busy traffic, for people who have more experience of cycling

- help working out a safe cycling route for a regular journey, such as to school or to work

- a simple map of local cycle routes, and suggestions for easy, enjoyable leisure rides (there is evidence that new cyclists generally start by cycling at the weekend for leisure)

- free cycle mileometer and DIY monitoring pack, so users could work out how they were doing

- a newsletter to encourage people to keep cycling, with lots of information about the benefits, especially losing weight, getting fitter and feeling healthier.

It would be great if we did this. And frankly, there is no reason we shouldn't. It would cost millions of pounds, but this would be little compared with the billions spent on road building, and the new cycling culture it could help stimulate would mean far less traffic in urban areas. It would be fantastic value for money.

* * *

The message from this chapter is that it is possible to rebuild a cycling culture in Britain. It will require a combination of soft activities to attract people who might never have considered cycling, and thousands of small-scale physical changes to make British streets as bike-friendly as those in Freiburg, Strasbourg and Winterthur. In Winterthur, I asked Herbert Ernst why they had put all this effort into cycling and he replied, "Because it is worth it."

"What should be the test of UK transport policy?" I was recently asked. After some consideration, I replied, "That children should be able to cycle where they want." A seemingly simple-sounding test, but a profound challenge to local councillors, government ministers and indeed to us all.

Chapter 7

Grand design:
the space between buildings

I first visited Phoenix, Arizona, in the 1980s, when my husband was working there. Ever since, the name 'Phoenix' has been shorthand for the unwalkable city in our household. My husband described the experience of trying to walk in Phoenix like this: "It takes ages and you don't find anything. It's like walking through one perpetual car park—parking lot after parking lot. When I first arrived I thought it was all one big car park. And pavements are in short supply to say the least. You don't see anybody if you're walking. People think you must either be a complete freak or extremely poor."

The overall fabric of our towns and suburbs is the outcome of hundreds of bad or good decisions, first about where new office blocks and shopping centres and housing estates should be located, and then about the functions of the spaces in between them. These decisions are in turn determined by the development plans or blueprints that politicians and planners draw up every few years. The locations of buildings, and how the space between them is used, have a great effect on how people choose to travel. If the fabric of our public spaces is wrong, the potential to entice people out of their cars is much less.

This chapter is about the choice between car cities, like Phoenix, public transport cities and walking cities. We will start on a whole city scale, looking at how the different types of city developed. Then we will examine the decisions that shaped Phoenix as compared with the city of Copenhagen, which has about the same population but a far smaller footprint. Finally, we will zoom in to see how much the design and location of a single housing estate or shopping centre affects people's travel choices.

Traditionally, European towns were structured on a walking scale. Until about 1850, the size of a town was limited by how far its inhabitants could walk within a reasonable time. It was rare for a city to be larger than about 3 miles across, the size at which it was possible to walk to the centre from a home at the city's edge in thirty minutes.[1] Walking cities were densely occupied, with houses, shops, offices, warehouses and industry jostling for space on narrow streets that wriggled and wandered according to the lie of the land.

With the advent first of horse-drawn trams, and then buses, bicycles, electric trams, metros and suburban trains, cities grew larger. Their citizens' daily travelling time stayed the same, but faster travel meant it was possible to commute further. The result was the public transport city, typical of urban areas built between about 1850 and 1950.[2] Public transport cities were often centred upon older walking cities, but they could be 10 to 20 miles across. Outside the older core, a fairly dense grid of streets spread out from main roads served by trams or trolleybuses. Train lines ran to outlying suburbs, and around each train station there was intense development of shops and houses. The train lines gave the public transport city the shape of a hand, with narrow fingers of intense development radiating from an inner 'palm'.

From 1950 onwards, growing car ownership made it possible for cities to develop in any direction, first filling in the gaps between the train lines and then spreading into the surrounding countryside. The palm and fingers pattern of the public transport city broke down and cities became blob-shaped, growing like amoebas to absorb villages which had once been distinct. Houses were built to low densities, with estate roads forming loops and lollipops which made walking distances long even where as-the-crow-flies distances were short. The road names changed too: instead of the Victorian-sounding Marquis Road or Albert Terrace, there are names like Hilltop Gardens, Beechwood Crescent, or Sycamore Close, which tell us something about the curving, discontinuous street layout as well as the semi-rural idyll to which the new occupants aspired, and often quite accurately describe the natural features destroyed to make way for the housing development. Shopping was no longer focused on traditional town centres or around suburban railway stations. Employment became spatially separated from housing, first in industrial estates and later in business parks or high-tech science parks. New motorways made it possible to commute from a home in one suburb to a job in another suburb of the same town, or even to a job in a suburb of the next town. The car city had arrived.

There are two important points about the way cities have evolved. First, the car city is a recent phenomenon. It has existed for a little over fifty years, as compared with the 10,000-year history of the walking city. As far as the history of humankind is concerned, it is an oddity, and one that our ancestors managed well without. In Europe, much of the urban landscape retains the characteristics of the walking city or public transport city, although that is changing.

Second, the transport that is available to people has a fundamental influence on city size and form, and this in turn determines the travel choices of its future inhabitants. For hundreds of years, it seems people have been willing to travel for an average thirty minutes to get to their work. The systems analyst Cesare Marchetti showed that the average land area belonging to Greek villages was 22 square kilometres, corresponding to a radius of about 2.5 kilometres, which is about the distance that can be walked in half an hour at an average walking pace.[3] The defensive walls around ancient cities commonly enclosed a similar area, allowing citizens to walk from the edge of the city to the centre in thirty minutes. Now, in the era of the car city, it takes us about the same time to get to work as it took Greek farmers to reach their fields many centuries ago—it is just that we travel faster and therefore further. The Australian researcher Jeff Kenworthy, who has spent many years investigating the links between the size and structure of cities and their transport, measured the average time it took for citizens of thirty-seven cities across the world to travel to work, and found that there was astonishingly little variation. The overall average was again thirty minutes. The shortest average journey time was about twenty minutes and the longest was forty-four minutes.[4] It appears we strongly but unconsciously adhere to a personal 'time budget', a budget for how much of our time we are prepared to devote to the act of getting about.

The transport that is available, and more especially its speed, determines where and how far we can travel in that magic thirty minutes, and hence it determines where people are willing to live. Cities are therefore shaped by the dominant transport mode of the era in which they were built. In turn, the form of a city determines the ease with which its future citizens can move around it by foot, by public transport or by car, and so affects their choice of how to travel. It is as though the travel patterns within a particular city, or part of a city, are frozen into its make-up at the time it is built. Today, we mostly walk in central London, as our ancestors did over 200 years ago. In the inner suburbs, we mostly walk or use public transport, again as our ancestors did about 100 years ago. And in the post-war outer suburbs, we mostly drive.

The moral is simple. There is little point in trying to entice people out of their cars, through persuasion and information and marketing, if we continue to build offices, homes and shops according to the car city blueprint. Of course, it is possible to walk to the shops from a house in a suburban cul-de-sac, but mostly, people will be disinclined to do it. Equally, employers moving to a new business park on the ring road can have some influence on their employees' travel decisions if they install bike parking and offer cut-price bus passes, but really it would be better not to move out to the ring road at all.

Towns are built by degrees. Occasionally, they undergo a massive spurt of growth, but most of the form of a city is decided by hundreds of small changes over many decades. Every time a bad decision is made—to build a business park or a housing estate or a new hospital or a shopping mall on green fields by a ring road, surrounded by car parking—the town becomes a little less walkable, a little less public-transport-friendly, and a little more car-dependent. The impact of one bad decision may be imperceptible, but the cumulative effect is large. In Chester, the county police headquarters is moving from the town centre to a new site on the outer ring road. In Newbury, the town planners gave Vodafone's world HQ the go-ahead on an edge-of-town site after the controversial bypass took traffic off the old road. In Norwich, the city-centre hospital closed and was replaced by a new hospital next to the city bypass. The hospital is difficult to reach without a car, so it needs more than 2,000 car parking spaces, which take up a lot of land. Locating the hospital by the bypass had a knock-on impact on other land use decisions: as well as new housing and a new access road, there will soon be a new research park next to the hospital, employing 10,000 people. Many of the research park's employees will live on the other side of the city—there are plans for 12,000 new houses there. How will people get from one to another? Via a planned new road, the Norwich Northern Distributor Route, that will link the out-of-town housing on one side of the city with the hospital and research park on the other side. In other words, because people have cars, the city is developing in a way which forces their use.

* * *

To see the logical end point of all those hundreds of bad or good land use decisions, it is worth looking at two cities of similar population which made some very different choices: Phoenix and Copenhagen.

Phoenix shows us what the car city looks like in its purest form. This is because almost all of the city's growth has taken place in the last fifty years, in the era of mass car ownership. In 1950, it was a small town with a population of just over 100,000 covering a land area of 17 square miles. Today, it is home to about 1.4 million people and sprawls over a massive 514 square miles (though the area it covers grows every year). In other words, it has roughly the population of Copenhagen spread across the land area of Greater London. Another way of putting this is that if Greater London had the same population density as Phoenix, it would sprawl far beyond the M25 motorway, swallowing Luton and Chelmsford in the north, and Guildford and Tunbridge Wells in the south.

Cars and roads define Phoenix, and you get a hint of the high priority attached to the car from the city government's official website, which proudly proclaims that Phoenix has 4,675 miles of road, 958 signalised intersections and 1,134 left-turn arrows. The idea of a city centre is fairly meaningless here; instead, low-rise offices, hotels and shopping malls are spread throughout the suburbs, along mile after mile of multi-lane highway. Drive-through ice-cream parlours, steak-houses and Mexican restaurants mean there is no need to get out of the car to order a takeaway. The suburb-to-suburb commute is the dominant commuting pattern.

During the period of Phoenix's rapid growth, there was little or no effort to concentrate development along public transport routes. The city's residents consequently have one of the lowest levels of public transport use in the world, on average getting on a bus or train slightly over once a month.[5]

Everything in Phoenix is spread out, but the amazing thing is that there is nothing in the spread; you can walk for an hour and get nowhere. In practice, most people do not walk much. The difficulties of walking anywhere in Phoenix are compounded by the fact that the city is built in the desert. Vast distances between buildings, no shade from street awnings or pavement trees, and the sun reflecting off acres of steaming tarmac and baking concrete make it a hostile city indeed for the pedestrian. With walking and public transport travel so difficult, it is not surprising to find that 93 per cent of all trips in Phoenix are by car and that the average Phoenix household drives over 17,000 miles per year.[6]

Construction of Phoenix's many miles of highways has come at a price. In the early 1990s, Jeff Kenworthy estimated the cost was roughly $400 per year for every man, woman and child in the city, which puts Phoenix at the top of the world league of big highway spenders.[7] In a country that prides itself on its low taxation, that is quite a lot of tax. You might hope that this huge price tag would at least mean Phoenix's residents were happy with their road system, but in fact a community attitude survey carried out by the city's government found that the two issues people were most likely to see as major problems in their neighbourhood were air pollution and traffic congestion.[8] Partly in reaction to that public concern, the city is planning a light rail line and cycle paths. It is committed to increasing urban density by building infill housing in the central area of the city; it wants new buildings to be pedestrian-friendly; and it wants new office and shopping development close to public transport stops to encourage greater public transport use. With great difficulty, one of the most car-dependent cities on Earth is trying to become at least a bit more of a walking and public transport city.

No doubt the Phoenix city planners in the 1950s and 1960s believed that they were building a utopian city, where anyone could get anywhere without the hassle and hold-ups that characterised old-world cities. Unfortunately, utopia proved to be elusive. To me, Phoenix feels more like hell on Earth.

Copenhagen lies at the other end of the spectrum from Phoenix. In contrast to Phoenix's extensive pattern of land use, development in Copenhagen is tightly concentrated in a fairly small central area, which has a population density about six times higher than the American city. Radiating from this central core, there are five development corridors, or fingers. In 1948, at about the time that Phoenix began its rapid growth, the people of Copenhagen had the foresight to adopt the idea of a 'finger city', and this is still the basis of the city's planning policies today. Just as in the traditional public transport city, central Copenhagen is the palm of a hand. The five fingers of development splay out from the palm towards the regional towns of Køge, Roskilde, Frederikssund, Hillerød and Helsingør. There is a train line along each finger, with trains every ten minutes from first thing in the morning until late at night. New housing, offices and public buildings are closely concentrated along the fingers, and especially around the train stations.

Despite the good public transport system, by the 1960s the centre of Copenhagen was coming under acute pressure from cars. Roads were clogged with traffic and many of the city's fine squares had been pressed into use as car parks. People began to feel that something had to be done to reclaim the city's streets. The Danish architect Jan Gehl puts it like this: "By the sixties, American values had begun to catch on—separate isolated homes and everyone driving. The city was suffering, so how could we reverse these patterns? We decided to make the public realm so attractive it would drag people back into the streets, whilst making it simultaneously difficult to go there by car." [9] The first step was the conversion in 1962 of the city's main street, Strøget, into a pedestrian street. That first step was highly controversial. People said that pedestrian streets would never work in Scandinavia, that there was no tradition of outdoor life, that 'Danes are not Italians'. Shopkeepers objected that they would lose trade because no one would be able to park outside their shops.

But the pedestrianisation of Strøget was a huge success, and it was followed by the creation of more and more car-free spaces. Over the next forty years, the car-free area in the centre of Copenhagen increased from 16,000 square metres to almost 100,000 square metres. Car parking was removed from 18 city squares. Every year, the number of parking spaces in the inner city was reduced by 2-3 per cent. At the same time, the network of bicycle lanes was extended, both in the centre of Copenhagen and alongside the main roads that run into the surrounding countryside. Now, roughly a third of Copenhageners commute to work by bike, a third by public transport and a third by car. Jan Gehl says: "Bicycling is once again a safe and rather uncomplicated mode of transport in Copenhagen, and it is not unusual to see the head of the Royal Theatre or a Minister of Parliament bicycling to work through the streets of the inner city." [10]

Copenhagen today fizzes with life. There are thousands of pedestrians walking along Strøget and the other car-free streets. Tables and chairs spill out from cafés and bars onto the street and are in constant use—even on chilly autumn evenings when the proprietors put out heaters and offer blankets to their customers. Wandering round the inner city, I came across one street which had been closed off to cars. A playground had been set up in the centre of the street, and parents sat on benches watching their children play on the slides. Elsewhere, there were buskers, jugglers and performance artists, and thousands of people sitting, strolling, window shopping and enjoying seeing and being seen. Instead of the noise of traffic, the sounds were of people talking, laughing and making music.

Jan Gehl has spent the last forty years documenting how Copenhagen has gradually changed, and his books have a fine collection of new and old photographs, showing Copenhagen as it is now compared with how it was. In the photographs of those same Copenhagen streets in the 1950s and 1960s, pedestrians are squeezed into two narrow pavements, with no room for pavement cafés or buskers. Cars sit bumper to bumper in the roads and squares. The most telling difference between the old photographs and the new ones is that in the old pictures, nobody is smiling.

The gradual process of reclaiming space formerly occupied by cars has had a profound effect on city life in Copenhagen, and Jan Gehl has been able to document this through three comprehensive studies of central Copenhagen, which measured street activity during the summers of 1968, 1986 and 1995. In each summer, he measured the number of square metres of pedestrian space and counted the amount of stationary activity—that is, the number of people sitting on benches or at pavement cafés, watching street artists, or window-shopping. Between the summer of 1968 and 1995, the car-free area in the centre of Copenhagen went up from 20,000 to 71,000 square metres, an increase of 3.5 times. The number of people using the street also increased 3.5 times. "Every time the city has expanded the pedestrian area by 14 square metres," he says, "another Copenhagener has turned up and set himself down to enjoy what the city has to offer." [11]

In Jan Gehl's conception, city streets are social spaces. They are not just movement corridors for getting from A to B, but places in their own right for all sorts of unplanned, unpremeditated, informal interaction with other people. The Australian environmentalist and campaigner David Engwicht feels the same way. The purpose of cities, he argues, should be to maximise the amount of 'exchange space' for talking, playing, watching the world and interacting with our fellow human beings. There is a trade-off between exchange space and mobility space: the more we have of one, the less we can have of the other. Cars are hungry for mobility space and use it inefficiently. If they are the dominant means of transport, the space they consume forces other uses out. [12] In Copenhagen, we can see what happens when this process is reversed and space dedicated to mobility is transformed into space for exchange. The new exchange space acts like a magnet to people, drawing them in to experience all the delights the city has to offer and creating a vibrant city culture which is free, spontaneous and diverse and in which anyone can turn up and take part. This would be unthinkable in a car city such as Phoenix.

When people look at cities like Phoenix and Copenhagen, they tend to imagine that they have 'always been this way'. But, as we have seen, central Copenhagen won back its public spaces from cars over a period of 30 years or more, and the process is still going on. Some people had a vision at the start, which included the finger city with a compact core as well as the idea that city centre streets should be the focus of public life, but the vision was not universally shared and many people were sceptical. Through a process of many small steps, Copenhagen's politicians, urban planners and activists were able gradually to persuade the sceptics that it was OK to get into the city by bike or by public transport, and that the social and economic benefits of taking cars out of the centre were great. Step by step, building on small successes, Copenhagen was transformed.

* * *

For any town or city, there is in the end a fairly simple choice: do you want to be a car-dependent town or a compact, bustling walking and public transport town? Every single decision about where new buildings should be placed, how people will access them, and how street space should be shared between different uses, takes us a small step towards one or the other of those two choices.

Having seen the cumulative effect of those thousands of individual decisions, and the way that, together, they build either a Phoenix or a Copenhagen, it is now time to put a few individual decisions—of the sort that might be made by a government regional assembly or the planning committee of a local authority—under the microscope. So, here are three common dilemmas, and some evidence to suggest what the effects of taking the right decision or the wrong one might be. The first dilemma relates to the design of new housing estates, the second to the location of housing, and the third to the location and scale of retail development. In each case, the property developers argue that doing things their way—the car-dependent way—is the only sensible option. They hope that the council planners will accept that 'these days, everyone drives' and that it would be perverse to reject a planning application that accommodates the inevitability of car use. The politicians and planners are frequently swayed by their arguments. And yet, in every case, there is an abundance of evidence to show that they are wrong, and that an alternative would be possible and better.

Dilemma 1: Must new housing estates be designed to cater for cars?

Suppose you are a planner or a politician in an area which is designated for housing growth. There is a plan to build a whole new community, of 10,000 or so new homes, as an extension of an existing town. The dilemma is that the developers want to build to a low density, with detached houses with double garages on curving and looping estate roads. They say that these days, people will drive most places, and that a more compact grid design would not have room for all the cars. Are they right, and is it inevitable that the new residents will drive? In that case, the blueprint for the new housing should allow for low housing densities, wide roads and plenty of space for parking and garaging. Or could a different housing design result in the new residents adopting less car-dependent lifestyles?

The best evidence relating to this first dilemma comes from a simple but elegant comparative study by two American researchers, Robert Cervero and Carolyn Radisch, which looked at travel patterns in two nearby neighbourhoods in the San Francisco Bay area of California.[13] They were interested in measuring how a neighbourhood's street layout affects residents' decisions on whether to walk, drive or take public transport. Intuitively, they thought that people might be more likely to drive if they lived in a low density neighbourhood where houses were spread out. They also thought that diversity of land use was probably important; that is, that people would drive more in monotonous neighbourhoods where houses were distant from shops, offices and workplaces, and would drive less in neighbourhoods which had shops and workplaces nearby. Finally, they imagined that driving would be more commonplace where the street design was pedestrian-unfriendly, and less common where streets were suited to walking.

They called these assumptions the three Ds: density, diversity and design. They had noticed that the three characteristics often went hand in hand. Older neighbourhoods tended to have high densities, diverse land use and streets that were well designed for walking; whereas newer neighbourhoods tended to be less compact, showed little diversity of land use and frequently lacked the pavements and safe crossing places that pedestrians need. So far, so obvious, but the really interesting question which they set out to answer was how much difference does it make? After all, the developers in our first dilemma are arguing that residents of high-density estates will drive just as much as their counterparts in spread-out housing.

The two neighbourhoods Cervero and Radisch investigated were roughly the same distance from the centre of San Francisco. Both areas were quite well off, with above-average incomes, and were seen as desirable places to live, with relatively high housing prices and rents. They had comparable public transport services and road access. In other words, in every respect apart from their physical layout the suburbs were extremely similar.

The first suburb, Rockridge, had grown up around the beginning of the twentieth century as a 'streetcar suburb' of San Francisco. Its streets formed a dense grid, and apartments and offices mingled with shops in the main shopping area at its centre. Cervero and Radisch described it like this:

"Rockridge is very compact, with mostly apartments and detached units with small yards and narrow sidelots. It features a finely grained and integrated mixture of land uses, in particular the very pedestrian-friendly College Avenue commercial district. . . . Storefronts are scaled to the pedestrian—shops are typically 40 feet or less in width, producing four or more shops on a typical block. Building entries open directly onto the sidewalk providing a nearly continuous sequence of showcase windows and shop entries. Many stores have loft apartments or offices above. Parking is accommodated on the street or behind buildings; few parking lots directly face College Avenue."

The second suburb, Lafayette, had been built after the Second World War and was much more car-orientated. Cervero and Radisch described it as Rockridge's polar opposite, with: "almost exclusively large-lot tract housing, curvilinear streets, and an auto-oriented retail strip and plazas."

"Mount Diablo Boulevard, the community's major thoroughfare, is 75 feet wide from curb to curb, with four lanes and a median strip over most of its stretch. Sidewalks exist in the commercial core, but are sporadic elsewhere. There is little mixing within land use zones, and no mixing vertically within structures. Retail is configured mainly along Mount Diablo Boulevard as stand-alone buildings with off-street parking fronting the arterial [highway]."

Cervero and Radisch collected information on travel habits from over 1,400 people in the two suburbs. The analysis of the travel data confirmed their 'three Ds' hypothesis. Rockridge residents walked and cycled more than people living in Lafayette, and they used their cars less. The difference was most dramatic for non-work trips—that is, going to the shops, the bank, the doctor or the cinema. For example, the people of Rockridge made 19 per cent of their shopping trips by foot, bike or public transport, while their counterparts in Lafayette made only 2 per cent of their shopping trips in this way. People in Rockridge made 17 per cent of their social and recreational trips by these green means of transport, compared with just 5 per cent in Lafayette. The average Rockridge resident travelled just under 11 miles per day by car for shopping, recreation and other purposes that were not related to their work. The daily non-work car mileage for the average Lafayette resident was nearly twice this, at 20 miles.

The difference between the people of Rockridge and those living in Lafayette was partly the result of Rockridge's more compact structure. Houses and shops were closer together, so some journeys were shorter and walking was easier. But Cervero and Radisch discovered that people's travel decisions were not simply related to trip distance. Even for journeys of the same length, people in Lafayette were more likely to drive. The researchers scrutinised non-work journeys of less than 1 mile, trips so short that they can easily be walked. In Rockridge, 28 per cent of these trips were made on foot. In Lafayette, the figure was just 6 per cent. People living in Lafayette were hopping in their cars even for a trip of a couple of minutes. The wide roads and lack of pavements made walking unpleasant, and perhaps the monotonous acres of car park instead of shop fronts made it boring and wearisome, too.

The story of Rockridge and Lafayette confirmed Cervero's and Radisch's hunch about the importance of the three Ds in shaping travel habits, and it provides the answer to our first dilemma. They showed that neighbourhood layout and design have a crucial influence on car use. Low-density housing estates with curving and looping estate roads, built miles from the nearest shops, can generate double the car use of housing estates laid out on a compact, 'old-fashioned' grid of roads. People's use of their cars varies a great deal, depending on how walking-friendly their neighbourhood happens to be. Housing developers and planners who assume that 'everyone drives these days', and who design accordingly, are making a self-fulfilling prophecy. They are designing in car dependency. A different approach could design in more sustainable travel choices.

Dilemma 2: Is it a good idea to build new housing in places with easy access by car?

Suppose you are a town planner considering a planning application for a housing estate. It is proposed for a site which has recently become accessible by car because it is close to the new ring road around the town. It is also convenient for the motorway. The dilemma is whether this is a good place for housing development—after all, the new residents will be able to travel easily using the ring road and the motorway. Does it make any difference to car mileage if a new housing estate is built close to a motorway junction? Would mileage be any lower in an estate that was built near a railway station? The clearest answer I have found to this question is in some British research, carried out by Carey Curtis and Peter Headicar.[14]

They were interested in recording the travel choices made by people moving into new housing estates. They investigated five estates in Oxfordshire, two close to Oxford and three on the edges of the small Oxfordshire towns of Bicester, Didcot and Witney. To understand the significance of their research it is first important to get a sense of these five estates and the places where they were built:

- The Botley estate was part of a residential suburb 3 miles from the centre of Oxford. It was close to the A34 Oxford ring road, but had frequent bus services into Oxford.

- The Kidlington estate was 7 miles from Oxford. Kidlington is a small dormitory town and also had frequent bus services into Oxford.

- The Bicester estate was close to the Bicester ring road and only a four-minute drive from junction 9 of the M40 London to Birmingham motorway.

- The Didcot estate was a short walk from a train station, which offered fast train services to London, Reading, Slough and Swindon.

- The Witney estate's distinction was that it was not close to Oxford, not near the motorway, and not convenient for train travel.

The researchers interviewed over 1,000 people in the five estates. They asked the new residents why they had moved house, where they worked, and how they travelled. One of the main reasons people had chosen the house where they were now living was to be 'close to work', but when Curtis and Headicar delved deeper they found that this apparently simple statement concealed a lot of complications. There was a large variation in the distances people travelled to work. Residents of the Bicester estate travelled on average 145 miles per week to and from their jobs. Those in Kidlington did less than half as much, 65 miles per week.

At first sight, the Kidlington residents were doing a lot better than the folk of Bicester at achieving their aim of being close to their work, but the explanation became clear when the researchers asked people how long their journey to work took. In all five estates, the average journey time was similar, at around thirty minutes. 'Close to work' did not mean close in terms of distance, but in terms of travel time. As in Cesare Marchetti's Greek villages and Jeff Kenworthy's 37 world cities, the residents of these five housing estates all planned their lives around the magic thirty minutes commuting time. The big mileage variation was possible because people in Bicester could commute a long way by car on fast roads within thirty minutes, and this is what they were doing: 95 per cent of them used a car to get to work. By contrast, most of the Kidlington residents worked in Kidlington itself or in nearby Oxford. Their average journey time was still thirty minutes, because many people used slower means of transport. They caught the bus, cycled or walked. Only 65 per cent of people living on the new housing estate in Kidlington travelled to work by car.

As estate agents say, what really matters in housing is 'location, location, location', and the research by Carey Curtis and Peter Headicar certainly demonstrates the dramatic impact of location on people's propensity to drive. The five housing estates can easily be ranked in order of decreasing sustainability. Kidlington was best, with 65 per cent of trips to work by car and the shortest commuting distances. The total car mileage per resident (for work and other trips) was 65 miles per week. This estate fostered sustainable travel patterns, because it was close to the major employment centre of Oxford and many people were therefore able to cycle or take the bus to work.

Next came Botley, with 73 per cent of trips to work by car and a total car mileage per resident of 97 miles per week. Like Kidlington, the Botley estate was close to Oxford and this meant that many of its residents were able to travel to work by sustainable means, especially by bike.

Ranked in the middle was Didcot. Here, 80 per cent of residents travelled to work by car but a good number commuted to work by train. The average weekly car mileage per resident was 102. Accepting that not all new housing estates in Oxfordshire could realistically be built next to Oxford itself, the Didcot estate was in a better location than those of Witney and Bicester. Although many of its residents drove to work, there were enough

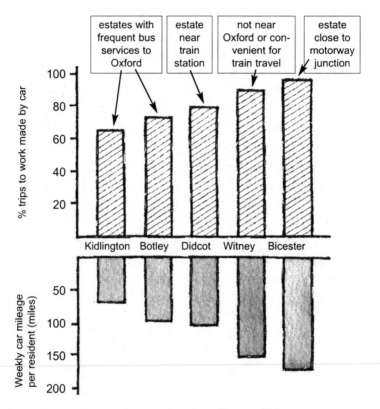

Figure 7: How housing location affects residents' car use.

people who chose to walk the few minutes to the station and commute by train to make Didcot's overall travel pattern a lot more sustainable.

Next came Witney, where 90 per cent travelled to work by car and total car mileage was 152 miles per week. The Witney estate had none of the natural advantages of the more sustainably located housing estates. Witney itself was not a major centre of employment, and for many people it was therefore a dormitory town, a place to sleep but not a place to work.

The worst estate was Bicester, with a massive 95 per cent of trips to work made by car and the longest commuting trips. Bicester had a weekly car driver mileage of 172 per resident, or more than 2.5 times the distance driven by the residents of Kidlington. The Bicester housing estate encouraged people to live heavily unsustainable lifestyles because it was built close to the motorway. Residents could travel at high speed to reach jobs that were many miles away but within the magic thirty minutes' acceptable commuting time.

The answer to the second of the dilemmas is clear: sites next to high-speed roads and motorway junctions are poor locations for new housing. The good locations are within a half-hour's door-to-door bus or cycle ride of a major town centre or within a few minutes walk of a train station on a line that connects to major centres of employment.

Dilemma 3: Now that most people shop by car, could more superstores reduce the distances we drive?

The rules on where big superstores may be built have become tighter in the last twenty years, but they are still lax and large retailers are still able to get planning permission for shopping sheds surrounded by acres of car park on the edges of towns. Build it big, stock thousands of product lines, and people will come from miles away. The latest retailers' trick is to build a mezzanine floor in an existing superstore, creating more space to stock with more products to entice more shoppers from further afield, and this can be done without even submitting a planning application.

This brings us to our final dilemma. Suppose a major retailer has submitted a planning application for a new superstore on the edge of town. The retailer points out that nearly everyone does their weekly shop by car nowadays, and claims that an extra store will actually reduce car traffic, because people will not have to drive as far to get to their nearest store. The risk that concerns you is that another superstore will take business away from neighbourhood shops, and that some people will end up driving a lot more.

So, does the retailer's claim hold water? It might do, if shoppers at a new store were simply transferring their custom from a more distant superstore to a closer one. But, as we saw in Chapter Two, superstores make their profits at the expense of smaller retailers. When a new superstore opens, smaller shops lose customers. These may be convenience stores or independent grocers, bakers, butchers and newsagents. Superstores are also expanding into non-food products and services like clothing, books, medicines and dry cleaning, and this is threatening yet more town centre and local centre shops.

Patrick Lingwood was interested in how people travel to local shops, and how the same people's travel habits change when a new superstore opens. He carried out a survey in a local shopping centre in north Oxford,

Summertown, which I know well as it was the place I shopped, on foot, as a graduate student. Summertown has two small supermarkets and about 100 other shops, which are a mixture of food shops, clothes shops, chemists, bookshops, banks, video stores, a post office and restaurants. It is a couple of miles from the centre of Oxford, and it is fairly typical of local shopping centres on the main roads out of cities across Britain. I lived near Summertown during the 1980s, before there was any competition from out-of-town superstores, and at that time over half (58 per cent) of Summertown shoppers came there to do their main weekly shop. The rest popped into Summertown occasionally for top-up shopping, to buy a newspaper or a pint of milk, but went somewhere else, such as Oxford city centre, for the main shop of the week.

Patrick's survey was carried out just over a decade later, in 1998, after a superstore had been built two miles away.[15] He found the superstore had a dramatic effect on people's shopping patterns. Only a little over a third (38 per cent) of Summertown shoppers still used Summertown for their main weekly shop. The rest came there for top-up shopping but did their main shop of the week elsewhere, most often at the new superstore. As Patrick put it, Summertown's role had changed significantly from predominantly 'main shop' to predominantly 'top-up' shopping.

As you might expect, trips to the new superstore were generally by car. Patrick found three-quarters of the big weekly shopping trips people made outside Summertown (mostly going to the superstore) were by car. However, the same people who drove to the superstore for their main shop tended to walk or cycle to Summertown when they wanted to make top-up purchases. Only a third of their top-up trips to Summertown were by car.

The people who did their main weekly shop in Summertown were even more likely to walk or cycle, and of these, only about a tenth arrived by car. For many, this was a conscious preference—that is, they owned a car and could have driven if they had wished, but chose to walk or cycle instead.

Happily, Summertown is still a successful neighbourhood shopping centre. However, other local centres have not been so lucky, and many have been destroyed by the growth of the superstores. Wherever there is still the possibility of shopping locally, it is important to provide protection against large-scale retail development. Patrick's evidence shows clearly that the opening of a new superstore abstracts customers from neighbourhood shopping centres. These people travel further to do their weekly shop than they did before, and are more likely to travel by car.

* * *

The message from this chapter is that it does not take long to change a city. A succession of apparently small planning decisions over twenty or thirty years can fundamentally alter patterns of land use. On its own, each decision might seem routine or inconsequential, but in fact the consequences of each badly sited or poorly designed housing development, and each edge of town superstore or business park, are huge. The cumulative effect of these many decisions will determine whether a town becomes sustainable—a public transport, walking and cycling town—or ever more car-dependent.

As we saw in the case of Copenhagen, towns, cities and regions must have a strategic vision to span that twenty- to thirty-year period. If every single land use decision is checked against whether it helps or hinders the achievement of that vision, a city can become a public transport, walking and cycling city more quickly than many of its citizens and councillors might even dare to hope. The choice of whether to become like Copenhagen or like Phoenix is ours.

Chapter 8

Why the political system cannot tackle transport

I once visited a senior civil servant in the Department for Transport to discuss what could be done about the growing levels of traffic on the roads. He was important enough to have a top-floor office of almost ministerial proportions (everything in government departments is carefully graded according to status), with a long mahogany table for meetings as well as a vast and curiously uncluttered desk. Sitting around the mahogany table, we were served real coffee in porcelain cups. The civil servant was the thrusting ambitious sort. He wore red braces and some people tipped him to be the next permanent secretary, which is the top civil servant post in a government department.

The discussion went something like this. We said that there was too much traffic on the roads, and that the Government ought to set targets to reduce it. He winced, rather as though someone had just made a rude noise at a well-to-do garden party. It was not actually the volume of traffic that was the problem, he insisted. Rather, there were a few unpleasant side effects of traffic growth, like congestion and pollution, and it was those that the Government was determined to deal with. We insisted that the problem was much wider than congestion and pollution. What about all the people killed on the roads, what about climate change, what about the way cars denied freedom to children to walk or cycle to their friends, and so on? All of these problems could be addressed if only the Government would agree to cut traffic, we said. Mr Red Braces replied that even if it might be a good idea to cut traffic levels, it was not actually possible. Then he said that even if it might be possible, the policies necessary to achieve it would not be politically acceptable. And finally, he said that even if it might turn out to be possible and politically acceptable, the policies needed to reduce traffic would have an unacceptable effect on 'UK plc'—that is, on the economy.

This response encapsulates several of the reasons why politicians and their officials have failed to address spiralling car-dependence. First, the class of people who run government departments are not typical of the population as a whole. At the more senior levels, they are disproportionately male and middle class, and relatively well-off. They are less likely to live in places blighted by traffic, because they can afford not to. They tend to travel by car and train, but not very much by bus. They are highly mobile and make more long-distance journeys than average. Consequently, they view transport policy through the windscreen. They simply do not see the wider problems of our car-dependent culture. People like Mr Red Braces become quite bothered and slightly hot about traffic jams—that is, congestion—but they are much less likely to empathise with the experience of an elderly person who cannot cross the road to collect their pension without help because the traffic is relentless, or with the person on the number 53 bus.

We are repeatedly told that traffic congestion is a big problem for the country. The Confederation of British Industry is obsessed by how many billions of pounds are wasted every year due to congestion, although the truth is that there is little basis in fact for the precise figures that it quotes. (The figures are calculated by imagining that all traffic is able to travel at the legal speed limit all the time, working out how many hours could thereby be saved by every man and woman, and multiplying this 'time loss due to congestion' by a notional 'value of time' measured in pounds and pennies. The calculation bears no relationship at all to actual money lost by businesses, for example because a delivery is delayed.) Not surprisingly, the constant harping about congestion plays on the public consciousness, so that in one recent government survey 92 per cent of the general public said that congestion was a serious problem for Great Britain.[1] But the curious thing is that rather few people actually feel that congestion is a big problem for them personally. The figures vary, but two recent surveys, again carried out by the Government, found that only between 22 per cent and 37 per cent of people believed that congestion was a serious problem on the journeys that they made regularly.[2] Repeated assertion of statements along the lines of 'traffic congestion is costing billions of pounds a year' has caused people to believe that it must be true, but the assertions bear little relation to people's everyday experience.

The Government expends a great deal of effort trying to remedy this 'problem' of congestion, despite the fact that not very many people are particularly worried by it. You might think that if a government is bothered about congestion, the obvious solution is to reduce the amount of traffic on the roads, while perhaps also making sure that roadworks are done promptly. Indeed, that is exactly what most other people think: yet another Government survey discovered that the top three causes of congestion that people mention are 'too many cars on the roads' (mentioned by six out of ten people); 'too many parents driving their children to school' (mentioned by nearly four out of ten people) and 'people driving with no passengers in their car' (again, mentioned by nearly four out of ten).[3] Despite this, the Government recently spent several years claiming that it could reduce congestion while allowing traffic to carry on growing. In its ten-year plan for transport, published in 2000, it suggested that congestion in big cities could be cut by 8 per cent at the same time as traffic increased by 10 per cent. In other words, people like Mr Red Braces thought we could have more traffic and less congested roads at the same time.

This nonsense was eventually abandoned, but still the idea hangs on that the priority is to deal with congestion, and that the other negative effects of car use do not matter half as much. This idea leads governments to put a lot of effort into things like better managed roadworks, advance information to motorists about congested conditions ahead, bigger road junctions, wider motorways, and, in London, congestion charging. The first two of these things are useful and sensible in the short term. The next two are definitely not sensible because the increased road capacity will attract more traffic and make the problem worse. Only the last of these policies, congestion charging, is effective in the long run, and this is because it gets to the core of the problem of congestion by cutting traffic. In doing so, it brings all sorts of other benefits: better conditions for cyclists and pedestrians, more timely journeys for bus passengers, less noise and pollution from traffic and so on. But so far, congestion charging has been implemented only by Ken Livingstone in London.

So, as Mr Red Braces explained to us, the first reason that governments have not done much to reduce car use and the resulting traffic growth is that they prefer to focus on a small and relatively unimportant symptom, congestion, instead of dealing with the underlying car-sickness.

The next reason Mr Red Braces gave us was that even if the Government wanted to reduce traffic, it is simply not possible, or at least not in a politically acceptable way. This is based on the assumption that, as society gets richer, more people will be able to buy cars, and once they have bought them they will inevitably use them. The only way to stop people using their cars is to impose sledgehammer restrictions—double the price of petrol, or put a tax on car parking spaces, or close roads—and this will cause public outcry, or so the argument goes.

This takes no account of places like Freiburg, where cycle paths and public transport have been given a high priority for the last thirty years and car mileage per household has consequently gone down. Nor does it tally with the experience in London, where investment in new bus services coupled with the central London congestion charge has reduced car use and commanded public support. Nor does it reflect the experience in Copenhagen, where a steady year-by-year reduction in the number of car parking spaces in the city has been acceptable because it has gone hand in hand with better streets for people to cycle and walk. These cities are living proof that it is possible to cut traffic through a judicious combination of attractive alternatives and gradual reductions in the space and priority given to cars. There is no need for the sledgehammer approach.

However, it is true that with the policies being pursued at the moment in most parts of Britain, it will not be possible to reduce traffic. This is because they are the wrong policies. If we did what Freiburg did, we could have dramatically better results. The problem is that the policies that are most effective in cutting traffic are rather subtle and gradual. They are not the sort of big-bang policies that most politicians like to be associated with.

Stephen Joseph, the director of environmental campaign group Transport 2000, put it like this: "Roads, and big infrastructure projects generally, have a totemic significance. Ultimately, politicians believe they need to be seen to be doing something." The macho culture of local and national politics means that councillors, county surveyors and politicians want to be associated with grand projects: building a bypass, or a bridge, or a tram or fast train line. For councillors and government ministers there is a touch of electoral vanity, a desire to cut the ribbon on something new and shiny to prove to the voters that you have done something important. For council officers and civil servants, it is careerism, showing that you are competent to manage a multi-million pound project in the hope that it will lead to promotion and to managing an even bigger and more prestigious one. 'Real' men (and it is usually men) do not see career advancement in doing small-scale stuff like building cycle networks.

This obsession with building big kit like bypasses, trams, bridges and fast trains was once described by the politician Steve Norris, in a moment of frankness uncharacteristic of a politician, as a political disease of 'grand-projectitis'. It does have to be said that this disease seems to afflict male transport planners rather more than women. A (female) local authority officer groaned as she told me about another big project in her town, where she felt city-wide cycle paths would have been much better value. "More toys for the boys" was the way she described the planned new tram. I apologise here for potentially offending half the readers of this book—but the truth is that decision-making about transport is male-dominated, and that in general, men seem to be more inclined to favour these large infrastructure projects, and that this bias causes a good deal of exasperation to many women and some, more enlightened, men.

There is also the difficulty that most senior officers in most local council transport departments were trained as civil engineers. They understand how to build physical things, made of concrete and tarmac, but they do not know how to work with local communities and businesses and schools to improve non-car options. Nor do they understand the process of enthusing people about the benefits of walking, cycling, car-sharing or catching the bus. Of course, they can employ people to do these jobs, and the better councils do, but jobs with titles like 'Sustainable travel co-ordinator' are generally on low salaries and short contracts, with little career structure and poor prospects for promotion to the senior and more powerful roles in the council.

Government funding rules mean that it is easier for local councils to get capital for large and expensive projects, like new roads and trams and bridges, than to get money for cheaper schemes like cycle paths and traffic calming. This is despite the fact that the 'benefit-cost ratio'—that is, the return that you can expect to get for your money, as measured by economists who ascribe a monetary value to every life saved or every second of motorist travel time avoided—is generally higher for schemes like traffic calming than it is for large civil engineering projects. It is also despite the fact that cycle paths and traffic calming can be spread right across a city, so that they bring benefits to every citizen, whereas a new tram line, no matter how good, benefits only those who live along or near its narrow corridor.

If money for small-scale infrastructure like cycle lanes is hard to come by, it is even more difficult to find the money for non-physical things, like more frequent bus services or information campaigns. The Government's logic is that the capital cost of building a new road or cycle lane is a one-off cost. Once it is built, that is an end to the financial commitment. In contrast, new bus services or information campaigns require an ongoing revenue commitment, which the Government is reluctant to make. In practice, this means that year after year, a local authority might spend millions of pounds on one large civil engineering project after another, but it does not have the option of stopping building these big pieces of infrastructure and spending the same money on an excellent bus service for its citizens and informing them of its timetable. If it tried to do this, the money would be taken away. Local authorities periodically find themselves with far more capital funding for civil engineering schemes than they know what to do with. As one (anonymous!) local authority officer once admitted to me: "We've got wheelbarrow-loads of cash at the moment. What are we spending it on? White elephant projects."

Grand-projectitis and inflexible funding rules are not the only things that militate against British cities adopting the policies of continental cities like Freiburg. Since the 1980s, British politicians have fought shy of any sort of strategic co-ordination of transport. Strategic co-ordination sounds boring, but it is essential. It means making sure that trains and buses are run as one synchronised system, so that they connect smoothly with each other. It enables bus lanes to be built from one side of a large city to the other, so that the whole bus network becomes reliable. It means being able to plan where new housing and office development happens, as in Copenhagen, so that it can be well served by public transport.

For strategic co-ordination to be possible, you need strong local government, with the power to co-ordinate and control transport across an entire region. This sort of co-ordination has been derided as 'nanny-statism' in Britain for nearly thirty years. Successive governments have taken the view that private companies are customer-orientated, thrusting and efficient and that the public sector is bumbling and incompetent. They have systematically set about disempowering the public bodies that should co-ordinate our transport services, taking away their ability to make transport better. Local authorities have no right to decide the overall shape of the bus network in their areas. They have little influence over train services. The bus companies and train companies may talk to one another to co-ordinate their services—or, on the other hand, they may not. If they do not, there is nobody with the power to bang their heads together.

Strategic co-ordination is viewed differently in other European countries. In Denmark, Switzerland, Germany and the Netherlands, public transport is run as a synchronised system. As we saw in Chapter Five, the regional or provincial governments in these countries have the power to say where and when buses, taxibuses and regional trains will run. They define the service and then contract with commercial companies to provide it. The result is a seamless public transport system that provides an attractive alternative to driving.

Stephen Joseph believes that there is a strategic planning deficit in the UK. The single exception he points to is London, where the Mayor, through Transport for London which he chairs, can decide what bus services should be provided, and how often they should run, across all 33 London boroughs. The Mayor decides what level bus and tube fares will be set at, and Transport for London operates a single ticketing system across all buses (run by about 15 different companies) and the tube. Transport for London also has the power to plan and improve the bus network, for example by installing bus priority lanes wherever they are needed along an entire bus route passing through several boroughs. Transport for London officers must consult with the boroughs, but they have a great deal of clout to make sure that strategically important projects, like a bus lane at a key pinchpoint, get done. Without these strategic powers, it would be impossible to boost public transport travel in London. With them, bus travel went up 40 per cent in just five years, so that Londoners made half a billion more bus trips in 2004 than they did in 1999.

"Strategic co-ordination is crucial to get better transport, and to get it, you need strong governance," Stephen Joseph told me. "Outside London, it's really difficult to do what London has done. Suppose you want a better bus service. To do that you need to have whole route modernisation, with bus lanes and so on wherever they're needed right along the bus route to stop the buses getting held up in traffic jams. At the moment the decision about a strategic issue like this can be sabotaged by an individual ward councillor whom five traders have lobbied because they don't want the bus lane outside their shops. The whole project disappears because the key bit of the bus lane has been rejected."

Across large conurbations, the absence of an overarching authority makes strategic planning next to impossible, especially if the different local councils have differing political complexions. Stephen Joseph pointed to another example: "There is a public transport co-ordinating body in the West Midlands, called CENTRO, but the different local councils in the region have different policies and they act against each other. So, for example, CENTRO and the local bus company Travel West Midlands might do deals on bus priority but Burton city council has conservative leadership that hates bus lanes and it's busy taking them out."

Stephen Joseph believes there is a solution to this problem. "There's an argument that we should roll out the London model to the other big cities," he explained. "You would have a Mayor for Greater Manchester with strategic planning and transport powers. The existing public transport co-ordinating body, which has rather limited control, would be given more powers, and would morph into a Transport for London-like body responding to the Manchester Mayor. It would then be able to start thinking strategically about things like bus priority and road-user charging, and do them conurbation-wide."

We are accumulating a lengthy list of reasons why the political system has failed to tackle transport: a deficit in strategic planning; an obsession with building big infrastructure; problematic funding rules; and a preoccupation with one small bit of the problem, congestion. But we are not finished yet. There is another reason, which goes back to Mr Red Braces' belief that action to cut traffic would be so painful that it would be political suicide for any government to pursue it.

Transport is a political hot potato. Any discussion about transport comes back sooner or later to the question of how to manage the growth in traffic, and that discussion is often understood as being about restricting people's freedom to travel by car where and when they choose. The people who become most agitated about this are those who rely on their cars the most, and those for whom a car is an important status symbol. They simply do not like the thought of driving less. Some of these people are newspaper editors or columnists, and they have made full use of their role in the media to paint any restrictions on driving as an affront to civil liberties. There is a good deal of hyperbole in their protests. Take columnist Simon Jenkins, writing in the London *Evening Standard*: "Muggers, gangs and burglars can roam free, but let one motorist stray an inch over a white line and the full force of the law will pounce in minutes." [4]

Accusations like this bear no relation to what really happens. Police enforcement of the speed limit is almost non-existent, and on motorways and 30-mile-an-hour roads more cars are driven at speeds above the legal limit than at speeds below it. [5] The introduction of speed cameras may have reduced vehicle speeds at a few locations, but on many roads speeding is so common that if you keep to the legal limit you will have a line of cars on your tail within minutes. Other forms of aggressive or dangerous driving are rarely prosecuted, and even when they are, the penalty is slight. The average fine for a motorist who has killed someone is about £200. The truth is that most motorists regularly break the law, and get away with it.

Nevertheless, vituperative attacks from the tabloid newspapers have scared off UK politicians. Government ministers are terrified that they may be accused of being 'anti-motorist', and this has made them reluctant not only to sanction more speed cameras, but also to promote traffic calming, encourage bus lanes and cycle lanes, which are resented because they reduce the space for cars, replace car parks with green parks or sitting space, or raise the tax on petrol to more closely match the huge environmental costs of its use. According to Stephen Joseph, "The top priority for transport ministers is to keep transport out of the headlines. It's very pragmatic—how do we do something that will immediately deal with the headlines we are going to get, and manage the system competently?"

I do not mean to suggest that a robust debate between people with different views about cars is a bad thing. The problem is that some newspaper editors only publish one side of the story, and quote selectively to back up that side of the story. A point of view that does not fit the editor's opinions does not get published. One freelance journalist told me that he was commissioned to write an article about cars and speed by a tabloid newspaper, but that when he filed it he was told that although (or perhaps this should be 'because') it was well written and highly persuasive, it could not be printed because it was not the editorial line. This particular example was from the tabloid press, but the supposed 'quality' press are not much better. In their motoring columns it is taken for granted that readers have the absolute right to drive around in a couple of tonnes of potentially lethal metal at speeds above the legal limit and with scant regard for other traffic rules, let alone for the collateral impact of their driving on the surrounding environment and communities.

But politicians should take some blame too. They have given up trying to explain the consequences of doing what the pro-car editors, journalists and interest groups want. When did you last hear the Chancellor of the Exchequer saying that a lower fuel tax will lead to more traffic, more pollution and worse climate change? When did a transport minister last explain that even the largest road-building programme conceivable, far bigger than we as a country can afford, will not reduce traffic congestion? When in the last few years did you hear them acknowledge that the growth in traffic is a problem? These big issues are simply ignored.

The pro-car line of the media bullies is not representative of what most people think. Opinion surveys show that most people feel that traffic growth is a bad thing. They also show that most people support action to improve alternatives to the car, even where this can only be done by making driving less attractive. In Chapter Three we saw some of the results of surveys that Werner Brög had carried out in the small town of Darlington. He also asked people there what they thought was likely to happen to the amount of traffic on the roads in the next five years. More than eight out of ten of the people he asked expected that traffic would increase, and more than seven out of ten said that they thought this was a negative thing.[6] Surveys in other towns show the same result.

Then Werner asked a very interesting question. "If we take action to favour sustainable modes, it will be to the disadvantage of cars," he explained. "If we act in favour of cars, it will be to the disadvantage of sustainable modes. Which would you prefer?" He found that more than eight out of ten Darlington residents favoured measures to help cycling, walking and public transport, even if these were to the disadvantage of cars. Less than two out of ten people wanted their politicians to improve conditions for cars at the expense of more sustainable forms of travel. Darlington residents are by no means unusual. A similar survey carried out right across the European Union in 1991 came up with the same result, with attitudes in Britain almost identical to the European average. So in fact it is not that the British citizen is somehow more backward than his or her Dutch or Danish counterpart in wishing for better transport provision. It is just that our media and politicians have failed to reflect or rise to the public's expectations.

Survey after survey tells the same story: people are more in favour of green transport policies than the politicians assume. A report about travel behaviour from the Organisation for Economic Co-operation and Development (OECD) includes three interesting examples of this: from Graz, in Austria, where the decision-makers believed that more than half of residents would oppose efforts to restrict traffic, but polls showed that the real figure was 15 per cent; from Leipzig, in Germany, where decision-makers thought 60 per cent of residents would like to see increased car use and less investment in public transport, but polls showed that only 5 per cent of residents agreed; and in the Netherlands, where decision-makers believed that only 14 per cent of residents would voluntarily agree to change transport modes, but polls indicated that 60 per cent would do so.

As the OECD report says:

> In Germany, for instance, employed males—representing only one quarter of the population, but three quarters of decision-makers—are much more likely to be car drivers than any other segment of the population. Their subjective perception of reality based on their experience as car-drivers may in many cases be quite different from that of the community at large. Examples from the Netherlands, Austria and Germany show that decision-makers can underestimate the willingness of citizens to restrict their car use and/or promote public transport by as much as a factor of four to ten.[7]

Of course, there is not unqualified public support for any action that will cut traffic. The context in which a question is asked is important. If asked "Would you like to pay more to use your car?" or "Would tighter parking restrictions help solve traffic problems?" most people will answer "No". Questions framed in this narrow way will almost always get a negative result. But the same people will answer differently if the question is framed in a wider context. "Would you support higher parking charges if we use the money to improve public transport?" and "Would you support closing the town centre to traffic so we can make it more attractive for pedestrians and shoppers?" are much more likely to get a positive reaction.

This issue of how a question is framed is crucial, both at the specific local level, consulting on whether to implement a new parking scheme or congestion charge, and for national politicians trying to explain the big choices we have in the years ahead. Stephen Joseph put it like this: "The problem at the moment is that the transport issue is talked about entirely in isolation. If you ask any group the question 'Would you like to pay more for motoring?' the answer will always be no. The question we should be asking is 'What kind of city do you want to live in?'"

In the next few years there will be a big public debate about whether drivers should be charged to use roads. "How the Government takes forward this public debate is critical," Stephen explained. "The only way to do it properly is to offer some real-world scenarios, which say here's how our cities are likely to develop on the business-as-usual model, increasing congestion and so on, and here are some of the things you can do about it. If we have a road-user charging scheme, here are some of the things we could do with the revenue from it. We could improve public transport and build more safe routes to schools, but we might also reduce council tax or business rates, or subsidise urban post offices, or even reduce fuel duty."

The public debate Stephen Joseph describes is a million miles away from the slanging match preferred by the tabloid media. It needs to be more subtle than 'cars bad; public transport good' (or the other way round, according to your viewpoint). It refutes the idea that environmental policies are hair-shirtish. Instead, we must make the case that policies which favour green transport over the car will give us nicer, cleaner, safer cities. The best way I have ever heard this put was by John Adams, a geography professor at University College, London:

"The political debate about transport is driven by an implicit opinion poll: 'Would you like to have a car?' Overwhelmingly, those without cars answer 'Yes!' They imagine the world as it is now but with themselves having access to the enlarged range of opportunities in life that can be reached in a car. This is the opinion poll to which most British politicians are currently responding. An alternative rendering of this question is 'Would you like to have your cake and eat it?'

"There is a second question that is rarely asked: 'Would you like to live in the sort of world that would result if everyone's wish were granted?' A possible alternative rendering of this second question is 'Would you like to live in a dirty, dangerous, noisy, ugly, bleak, brutish, socially polarised, fume-filled greenhouse?' The answer to this question is obvious.

"But reducing our dependence on the car is not only necessary, it is positively desirable. There is a third question: 'Would you like to live in a world that is less dependent on the car?' An alternative possible rendering of this question is: 'Would you like to live in a cleaner, quieter, more peaceful, beautiful, harmonious and neighbourly world?' Such a world is possible.

"The challenge is to put the second and third questions on Britain's political agenda. The choices we make frequently depend on the way the questions are put." [8]

Mr Red Braces gave one last reason for the Government's reluctance to deal with the growth in traffic. He said that the policies that are needed to cut traffic would be bad for the economy. The logic behind this assertion requires a bit of unpacking. Over the last fifty years, the rate at which traffic has grown has closely mirrored the rate at which the economy has expanded. During times of recession, when the economy is static, there is little traffic growth. During times of expansion in the economy, traffic grows faster. The reason for this relationship is straightforward: higher economic growth means that people have more money to spend on travel, as well as on everything else. When the economy is booming, more people have the money in their pockets to buy a car, more people can afford the extra petrol for optional trips, and people and businesses buy more, too, which means there is more freight traffic.

But there is no reason why this historical relationship between economic growth and traffic growth should carry on for evermore. Although the amount of money in people's pockets clearly has an effect on how much they travel, it is not the only thing that influences car traffic levels. If there are good alternatives to driving, car owners will be more inclined to leave their vehicles in the driveway. In other European countries which have better public transport systems than Britain, people use their cars less. Good public transport can also relieve people altogether of the need to buy a first or second family car.

So the economists are starting to talk about the possibility that traffic growth and economic growth might be 'decoupled'. In 1996, the Government asked its own committee of economic advisers to consider whether this might be possible. Sitting on the committee were four top professors from the field of transport economics, as well as Michael Roberts, the Head of Industrial Policy at the Confederation of British Industry and Stephen Joseph from Transport 2000, who both brought a bit of real life to the committee's sometimes theoretical and abstruse discussions. The committee took three years to do its job. In 1999, the Government published the result: a hefty 300-page report, *Transport and the Economy.*[9]

Looking worldwide, the advisers concluded that growing national income could only explain part of the growth in traffic, and that other factors were important too. They pointed out that there was a large variation in car kilometres per $1,000 of Gross Domestic Product (GDP) between different countries. Even within Europe, this varied from a low of 213 car kilometres per $1,000 GDP in Spain to a high of 430 car kilometres per $1,000 GDP in Finland. The figures outside Europe varied even more. Of the fifteen European countries for which they had data, the UK had the fourth highest car kilometres for a given level of economic activity. The committee also noted that Britain had lower levels of car ownership than some other European countries, but rather high levels of car use: for example, British car kilometres per person was almost the same as in Germany, despite car ownership being only three-quarters of the German level. In their words, there could be "a significant degree of variation in how much traffic will arise from any given level of national income. This leads us to conclude that policies intended to change the volume of traffic that will arise from any particular level of economic activity are, in principle, feasible."

The next question for the committee was whether traffic reduction policies would have a good or bad effect on the economy. They concluded that in some circumstances, carefully designed traffic-reduction policies can actually increase economic welfare. In other words, traffic reduction might be good for the economy. This is exactly the opposite of the conclusion reached by Mr Red Braces. The committee cautioned that their conclusion would only be true where the full environmental and social costs of car traffic are not being paid by car drivers. That is, if it were possible to add up the cost in pounds of all the road deaths, pollution, noise and other damage caused by car traffic, traffic-reduction policies would be good for the economy so long as these so-called 'external' costs were bigger than the actual cost of driving. Most economists who have tried to quantify these external costs believe that drivers pay much less than the true environmental and social cost of their travel. So carefully designed traffic reduction policies could be good news for what Mr Red Braces called 'UK plc'. The committee also pointed out that some traffic-reduction policies, like congestion charging in cities, could raise quite large amounts of money, and that these could be recycled for the benefit of the whole community.

These macroeconomic arguments are all very well, but they do not tell us much about the effect of traffic-reduction policies on the local economy. Businesses, especially small high-street retailers, often oppose policies such as congestion charging, parking restrictions, pedestrianisation or a new bus lane past their shops, because they believe that these policies would be bad for trade. They argue that policies like this will send shoppers elsewhere, to out-of-town shopping centres with acres of free parking, or to neighbouring towns with fewer traffic restrictions. So what is the evidence about these more local economic effects?

When Oxford City Council decided in 1999 to close some city-centre roads to traffic, it faced a storm of opposition from businesses that claimed the changes would drive shoppers out of the city. The campaign against the road closures got onto national television several times, and

filled the pages of the local paper. Despite the controversy, the city council went ahead. It pedestrianised two shopping streets, and closed the surrounding streets to most vehicles except delivery vans, taxis and cars
belonging to city-centre residents. Because retailers were so adamant that
the changes would kill their businesses, the council agreed to monitor the
economic impacts of the scheme. Two years after the road closures, property and retail consultants C. B. Hillier Parker reported back. They found
that, far from deterring shoppers, the changes had actually attracted more
of them. The number of pedestrians in the streets with traffic restrictions
went up by about 9 per cent. Rents for prime retail sites—a good measure
of the vitality of a shopping centre—held steady in Oxford, despite a general downturn in rental values in other towns in the south-east of England.
Traffic coming into the city centre went down by about a quarter, and the
number of people travelling in by bus went up.[10]

The Oxford experience is repeated time and again. Often, the reclaiming of a city centre from cars is so successful that local businesses shift
from their initial hostility to demanding that the scheme be expanded.
This is what happened in York, where, in the late 1980s, the city council
decided to close some city-centre streets to traffic. At first, they faced
strong opposition from retailers, who said that if cars were no longer
allowed into the centre, it would kill their businesses. What happened was
exactly the opposite of what the shopkeepers had predicted. The number
of pedestrians in the newly traffic-free streets doubled. Shop rents grew
faster in the traffic-free streets than in surrounding streets which had not
been closed to cars, and retail turnover in York went up compared with
similar British cities. The retailers were won over. They stopped arguing
that cars should be let back into the city centre, and started saying that the
traffic-free zone should be expanded.[11]

Shopkeepers in Oxford and York are typical of retailers everywhere.
They assume that most of their trade comes from people in cars. They
think that bus passengers, pedestrians and cyclists are poor customers,
unable to carry much away and too poor to have a car, and therefore with
little money to spend. When cars are excluded from the town centre, these
shopkeepers expect that trade will suffer. The reason that their expectation
turns out to be wrong is that their assumptions about their customers are
generally inaccurate.

Think for a minute about a local shopping centre—not a bustling city
like York or Oxford but a suburban town centre on the outskirts of a large

Count the shoppers! When York City Council decided to restrict traffic, the number
of pedestrians using the newly traffic-free streets doubled.

conurbation—somewhere like Eltham, Harlesden or Harrow in outer
London. These are the sort of places where there is a lot of traffic on the
roads. Walking to the shops is not very pleasant, because of the noise and
fumes. Buses are regularly held up in traffic jams. Now, how many of the
shoppers there do you imagine have arrived by car? And what proportion
of the money spent there is from car-borne shoppers? 80 per cent? 40 per
cent? 20 per cent?

The answers are surprising. On average, less than a fifth of shoppers at
a typical outer London suburban town centre travel there by car. The
rest—nearly four-fifths—arrive on foot or by bus, with a tiny number
coming by bike, train or taxi.[12] Many of the shoppers who arrive by bus
or on foot have a car available, but choose not to use it. The spending profiles of the different types of shopper are quite similar: car drivers spend
slightly more per trip, but they visit less often. Hence, the average weekly
spending of a car driver in one of these suburban town centres is £75,
compared with £66 for an average bus passenger and £88 for someone
who has walked. Astonishingly, more than £8 of every £10 entering the

tills at these suburban centres comes from the purses or wallets of shoppers who have walked or caught the bus or train. Less than £2 in every £10 is spent by car drivers.[13]

Knowing these figures, it starts to make sense that the best way to boost a local shopping centre might be to make it a more attractive place, with wider pavements, street cafés, and less traffic noise and fumes. If this means excluding cars, it is not such a big deal. Car-borne shoppers make a rather small contribution to the economy of the town centre. They are not the crucial ingredient that keeps businesses alive. And, of course, if the town centre is spruced up and bus lanes are put in, some of those car-borne shoppers will leave their cars in the garage and catch the bus into town. Town centres cannot compete with out-of-town superstores in terms of convenience of car access, but they can beat the superstores in creating places where people actually want to be. In fact, this is the only way they can win. Trying to beat the superstores at their own game is doomed to fail.

So Mr Red Braces' final excuse for inaction does not stand up to scrutiny either. It is possible to reduce traffic levels without damaging the economy of a town. We can even say that it is essential to reduce traffic levels in order to let a town thrive.

* * *

Our politicians bear a heavy responsibility for our society's failure to deal with car-sickness. The political class, including civil servants, journalists, pollsters and pundits, as well as the people we have elected to represent us, almost invariably sees transport policy through the windscreen, and they have consequently misunderstood the nature of the problem. They think that the top priority for us, the people to whom they are supposed to be accountable, is to be able to drive wherever we want, as fast as we can, with no impediment. In moments of clarity, they know that they cannot deliver this, and could never do so, no matter how much money they had to spend and however powerful they were.

The double tragedy is that, as we have seen, this is not what most people actually want, and the thing we do want—in John Adams' words, "to live in a cleaner, quieter, more peaceful, beautiful, harmonious and neighbourly world"—is entirely possible. To deliver that world does not require the implementation of restrictive policies that would be electorally unpopular. Far from it. The actions of towns like Freiburg and Copenhagen, and the evidence we have examined throughout this book, from Aarhus to Winterthur and from Aylesbury to York, shows that it is both possible and popular to live in a world that is less dependent on the car. The cure for car-sickness is so easy and so obvious that decision-makers, searching for a solution that is both expensive and dramatic, simply cannot see it.

Chapter 9

Learning not to drive

Not many people manage to live without using a car at all—at least, not in developed countries, where life has been rebuilt around motorised transport in the last fifty years. Living in a rural area of Wales, we have decided not to own a car and instead I catch a lot of buses and trains, own three bicycles—each one suited to a different sort of trip—and walk in all weathers. But I still regularly use vehicles of one form or another. I take taxis; from time to time we hire a van to move heavy loads; and we belong to a car club which gives twenty or so neighbours the shared use of three cars. The food I eat, the clothes I buy, the couriers delivering parcels and packages to my office, and the deliveries of plasterboard, windows and other building supplies to the house that my husband is building for us, add up to a lot of motor transport. I try hard to keep my use of cars to a minimum, while knowing that I cannot manage without them altogether.

This chapter is about individual actions to lessen car use. These individual actions are mostly very easy and obvious things to do, which follow quite straightforwardly once you have decided that you would like to be less dependent on a car.

Most people do not want to take the responsibility for their car use. In the course of writing this book I had many conversations with friends about cars and our society's dependence on them. After a while, it became clear that there was a pattern to the conversations. They went like this:

Friend: What's the book about, then?

Me: Well, it's about the problems caused by so much car use, and the solutions. It's about the way that the people who run the transport system are fixated on big-bang civil engineering projects and see transport as a technical problem, whereas really it's a social problem. I think we need to change the way we use cars.

Friend: Hmmm . . .

Me: A lot of the time, people drive from habit, and don't even consider what the other options might be. . . .

Friend (interrupting): The problem is that the railways are in such a mess. My mother came to see us recently, and the train was late, so she missed her connection, and then the train she finally caught didn't have the air-conditioning working and it was like a furnace in there. The windows wouldn't open. And the toilets were disgusting. And by the time she got here she was in such a state. You really can't expect people to travel like that.

Me: Well, no, of course not. That's awful. I know what you mean about that train. But the point is that for most people, there are journeys that they could as easily make without driving—you know, by bike, or walking, or sharing a car with someone else. Often it's the short trips—more than half the car trips people make are short enough to cycle.

Friend: I couldn't possibly let Ben cycle to school. The traffic's terrible. Everyone drives at about sixty through the village. Anyway, living here, you've really got to have a car. I need it to get to work. . . .

The friends who say these things are often very environmentally aware in other areas of their lives. They recycle their glass and paper; they buy low-energy light bulbs; they prefer organic fruit and vegetables and avoid tropical hardwoods; some of them work for environmental organisations. They are able, thinking people and have been prepared to make changes in their lives because of their concern about the global and local environmental damage that they see being caused by human beings. They consider themselves to lead green lifestyles.

Many of us are aware that our reliance on cars is causing the climate to change. We know about the destruction of the countryside caused by road building. And yet it is so much easier to put the responsibility for resolving the problem onto someone else—the Government, or the train companies, or the local council—than to take a share of the responsibility yourself. "If only there was a decent public transport service," the argument goes, "then we wouldn't need to use our cars. But until public transport is better, there is nothing else for it—we'll just have to drive."

Of course, it is true that the trains in Britain are often late, over-crowded, and ill-ventilated in summer. Some train journeys are hideously expensive, certainly in comparison to train travel in Europe. Services do not connect. It is also true that many main roads are terrifying for cyclists, and not at all suitable for a young child cycling to school. The people in charge of transport have served us badly.

But even if they had served us better, the transport planners would not have been able to create a public transport system that provided for all the journeys we currently make by car. There is something wrong with our expectations. We are entitled to expect a better public transport service, and to argue for it, but we are also obliged to take responsibility for our own travel choices. A car may be essential sometimes, but not always. Even allowing for the inadequacies of public transport, a good proportion of car journeys could be made perfectly satisfactorily in another way.

Many people who think of themselves as environmentalists still have a blind spot about cars. For David Engwicht, the Australian environmentalist, the realisation that his travel patterns were in contradiction to his personal values came when he was fighting against a freeway through his Brisbane suburb. He says: "This struck home to me in the middle of the Route 20 battle, when I realised that my use of the car had increased dramatically as I raced around having brochures printed, making arrangements and going to meetings. I was fighting a freeway by using a car more. I did the only thing I could—bought a bike." [1]

Most people will not have such a sudden realisation, but instead a growing feeling that it would be good to drive less. Here are three stories about people who have limited their car use, why they have done it, and how it works. All three of them live in small towns or villages in a rural area, and they all have children at home—both factors that are commonly used to justify high car use.

Karen R. lives with her partner and three-year-old son Janoš in the little west Wales village of Bethania, nearly 10 miles from the nearest town. Bethania is a sleepy place, and you might think that Karen needs a vehicle more than most people, to get to the shops, to take her son to playgroup, to get out. But they have decided not to own a car. Karen's perception of the choice they have made is a positive one: she feels her life without a car is more sociable, and that it offers more freedom to her son. She puts it like this:

"Not having a car, you get so much more contact with people and the land. You see and experience things so differently. It seems to us that people glide across the land in a car rather than really connecting. I've seen it happen with children especially. They're carried in these plastic car seat carriers and people hardly seem to take them out. They carry these things around, they go into a shop or café or someone's home and the child is plonked on the floor in this plastic car seat and then they get picked up and put into the car and taken to the next port of call.

"We went up to meet someone from the bus on Tuesday and we know the three bus drivers. We know them all, and they know these people are going to see Christopher and Karen. Another neighbour was on the bus. There are a lot of connections! You meet people on the bus and you meet people when you walk to the bus. You don't if you're in a car.

"Long distances we'd never want to do by car anyway. We go by train because we all enjoy it as much as anything else. My child has been going on the train since he was born and he loves trains! It's partly because he is used to it; but travelling by train is much easier . . . They're much less confined, they don't have to sit in a car seat, they're not strapped down, they can walk up and down the aisle if they want to, they can look out of the window. With some car seats for kids, they can't actually see out of the window very easily. They certainly can't move around and they can't sit on your lap. It's infinitely better by train, as far as I can see."

Because Karen mainly uses public transport, she organises her time differently from car users. Whereas families with cars find themselves running hither and thither every day of the week, Karen plans so that several things are accomplished in one journey. This is particularly necessary because the bus service from Bethania is infrequent. The way she plans her journeys gives more time to do special things with her young son, compared to other families she knows. "The bus service means that we have to stay several hours in town, so we have to find things to do. That's pretty easy if you're fairly organised. We do things with Janoš and we shop and we meet people. We usually combine all that stuff on one day a week. We use the library, we go to the museum, we do things like that, which other people would not do. We've been on shopping trips with neighbours from time to time and it's quite uncomfortable because it's quite different—get out of the car, do the shopping, get back in the car, go home, and we say, well what was all that about? What happened? We're just used to taking our time."

Other people worry about how to carry the shopping without a car, or what it would be like to go on holiday by public transport, especially with a three-year-old in tow, but Karen does not find either of these things difficult. She has found practical solutions which work for her family. Most of the family grocery shopping is bought in bulk from a wholesale company which delivers in the area every fortnight. Karen buys tinned foods and dry foods like cereals, pasta and flour this way, although perishable foods are not delivered. "We've managed by getting stuff wholesale. Then when we go shopping we have rucksacks and we carry things. I find with a rucksack and maybe one bag, I can do a weekly fruit and veg shop. And if Janoš needs to go on my shoulders, he does. The only shopping that is an issue is the big things and often those wouldn't fit in a car anyway—things like fencing, or big equipment—and so we get those things delivered.

"When you go away, you have to be quite organised with your packing; you can't throw everything in the boot of the car. We go away for three or four weeks and we take everything in our rucksacks. Our only constraint over Christmas was not being able to take back all of Janoš's toys, all the mountains of toys people had given us without thinking how we were going to get back."

Karen has also bought top-quality carrying equipment, some of it second hand. "With a young child a good backpack carrier is useful. That's a really good investment," she told me. "You need a rucksack and a good buggy. And train your children to walk! It's so important for kids to walk and a lot of children don't. They get ferried around and the only exercise they get is sport."

When I asked Karen what advice she would give to a family that wanted to cut their car use, she was uncompromising. "I think you just have to get rid of it! Throw away the keys! As long as the car is there you're going to use it."

* * *

Karen's feeling that life without a car is more sociable is shared by Teresa W., the second person I spoke to. Teresa lives in Borth, a little seaside town. She has two teenage children, an eighteen-year old son and fifteen-year-old daughter. The children live half of the time with Teresa, and half of the time with their father, who has a house nearby. Teresa described the benefits of being car-free like this: "If you ride a bike, you wave at people as you go through the village. On the train I meet the same ten people every morning. You chat, and then you sit on the train with people that you know because you go on the train to work every day. I walk into Aberystwyth to do my shopping and catch a bus back and I meet people on the bus. The children are the same because they go everywhere by public transport."

What Teresa appreciates is the chance for impromptu social contact, which would not happen if she drove everywhere. She also likes the way it has made her children more independent: "They have travelled pretty much independently since they were about eleven, locally. If you've got a car you have no excuse not to drive them everywhere, because one wants to go to ballet and violin lessons and the other one wants to go to football and tap dancing. You've got no excuse to say no. But if they've got to go on the bus, it's different. If they can organise it themselves, they can go."

Teresa uses her ex-partner's car about once a fortnight. This works well, because they are good friends and have worked out a fair arrangement. "I pay the tax and help with bills to some extent. I make sure there's extra petrol in the car when I've used it, and he adds me to his insurance." She pointed out that this sort of car sharing, where one person owns the car and someone else has occasional use of it, is easier with someone you know very well. It does not always work: "I've been in a car-share scheme before where we worked out a mileage rate to use someone's car. I wasn't ever sure whether they were happy, whether they thought they were charging enough." This time, though, the arrangement is successful. The lesson seems to be that this kind of car sharing is more suited to family or close friends—people you know would tell you if they were unhappy with the deal.

Occasionally, Teresa hires a vehicle—usually a van when she has to transport something that is large or heavy. "I recently picked up a sofa and I hired a van. Hiring a van now and again makes a lot more sense than having a vehicle that I don't want sitting outside my house all the time, rusting."

Teresa lives 15 miles from her work. She used to work from home most of the time, but that changed a few years ago, and now she commutes to work by bike or train. She likes to keep fit, and cycling to work is one way of building some exercise into her routine. "I tend to cycle one way and take the train the other depending which way the wind is blowing. Some days I cycle both ways, some days I go on the train both ways if it's really disgusting weather or I'm in a hurry." The trains between home and work only run every two hours, but she has turned this to her advantage: "I have a very quiet start to the day—get on the train at seven-thirty, get into work before eight, start work at eight, have a quiet hour."

Her work involves a lot of meetings and being out and about, and again she tries to schedule her working day so that she can get to these meetings by public transport. "I very rarely drive for work purposes because you can get nearly everywhere by public transport if you're prepared to walk a bit. I've got access to all of the timetables. Most people are flexible about when you meet. It might be 9.30, it might be 10 a.m. It might definitely have to be Thursday morning but it can be any time within a couple of hours. I'll book it in to suit the public transport. So using a car for work is very rare and that's quite important to me because people need to see that it's possible. It's much more fun! And I can work on my way to my meetings rather than just driving."

Teresa joked that she has to buy a lot of food. "A lot of my income goes on food—I have to eat more, cycling everywhere!" With an eighteen-year-old and a fifteen-year-old in the house too, I wondered if the weekly shop posed some problems for her. "The concept of a weekly shop is a very car- and supermarket-oriented concept," she explained. "If you don't have a car, you don't do a weekly shop, you do a daily shop. You get stuff that's fresh; you don't get so much stuff that's in tins and bags because they're heavy. You get more beans and things from the wholefood shop that you can add water to later. There are a couple of corner shops, grocery shops, in Borth and there's the Wednesday market where I work and two market gardens that I pass on my way home. I probably spend about twenty minutes a day shopping one way or another. Every now and again I'll go and stock up with things like tins of beans that you can only buy in supermarkets, but I tend to do lots of little shops every day."

Living in the same rural, highly car-dependent area as Teresa, I am conscious that if you do not own a car, it can be a nagging doubt that you are not playing a full role in society. The problem is not one of opportunities forgone, but a worry that if you accept lifts from other people—even occasionally—they might feel that you should be able to offer lifts to them too. I asked Teresa how she tackled this. "I don't tend to ask people for a lift. I only accept graciously if they offer, unless they're friends or we've got an arrangement about sharing cars and then I ask. If someone gives me a lift, I will always pay the petrol, or buy them a drink, or drive them home in it if I'm insured . . . whatever it is that helps. Maybe they'll drive and I'll buy the tickets. If there's something good on and someone's taking a car full of kids, you don't have to feel that next time you necessarily have to drive those children somewhere. You could do something else—have them over on a Saturday morning, or take them to something else that doesn't require a car."

Teresa's reasons for minimising her car use are complex and interesting. At one level, her reasons are altruistic: she is strongly aware of the environmental benefits of using cars less, and of wider benefits to the whole community: "I'd prefer to see my money going to the local grocer's shop, to the local market garden and to the local organic vegetable shop, rather than to the petrol station, because I don't think much of the money that goes to the petrol station is going to stay locally. Whereas with the grocer's and so on, I think a lot of the money will stay in the local economy." But she is also honest enough to admit that she would not adopt a low-car lifestyle purely for altruistic reasons. The big personal advantage of not running a car for Teresa is that it saves a lot of money, which in turn enables her to work part-time: "There's a financial thing as well. If I ever wanted to run a car, I'd have to work full-time to pay for it. Instead I work 2½ days a week and don't run a car. It's hard to put my motives in a hierarchy. I wouldn't exactly say that I don't have a car because it saves me money but I would say that not having a car helps me work a really short working week and that makes life very, very nice. And I really like the rest of my life. I'm not selfless enough to give up a car solely for environmental reasons. It has to benefit me and it does that by me not having to work so much. I have more time to do what I want to do because I don't run a car."

Her comment unconsciously echoes the point by Ivan Illich with which this book began. The costs of running a car are a lot higher than people realise. A typical car driver on an average salary has to work nearly two days per week to earn the money to buy a car, garage it, and pay for petrol, insurance, repairs and parking. By contrast, Teresa's weekly expenditure on public transport can be earned in about an hour.

I asked Teresa what her advice would be to someone who wanted to cut their car use. "Get a Gore-Tex jacket, buy a train pass, set up a carshare scheme, and stop worrying about detail, your appearance, being a bit sweaty. Try to encourage your employer to make it doable, with things like showers and bike racks and encouragement for going to meetings on bicycles." She also believes that small lifestyle changes by individuals could have a wider impact, encouraging others to reconsider their own car use: "Make people more aware of it so that it becomes acceptable. Economically, socially and culturally and obviously environmentally it's totally acceptable, but people's commitment to reducing their impact sometimes seems to be less than their commitment to having a nice hairdo, which is remarkable in a way."

* * *

The last of our three non-car owners is Andy R. He is a member of the informal car club in Machynlleth to which my husband also belongs. Car clubs are relatively new in Britain, but well established in Switzerland and Germany and beginning to take root in America. The idea behind a car club is that a group of people share the use of several vehicles. Members do not have to pay the large up-front cost of car purchase, but instead pay a fixed rate per mile they drive. Some car clubs also charge people an hourly fee, although this does not happen in the Machynlleth car club. The mileage and hourly charges are set to cover the cost of car purchase or leasing, insurance for all the users, repairs, petrol, tax and so on. In the larger, professionally run car clubs, the charges must also cover the cost of staff to manage and publicise the scheme. In Machynlleth, members of the car club pay 30 pence per mile, with no membership fee and no hourly fee. This has the beauty of simplicity—everyone knows exactly how much their trip will cost.

Perhaps counter-intuitively, car clubs are an effective way to reduce car use. The pay-as-you-go system means that car-club members are more aware of the cost of using a car. This makes it easier to compare the cost of driving with public transport fares, so car club members tend to mix and match their travel, using a car when that is the most appropriate option, but cycling or catching the bus or train for other trips.

Andy explained how the Machynlleth car club works. "If you want to do a journey, you book it on the chart." The chart hangs on a nail in the side passage between two of the members' houses, so any member can check at any time whether there's a car available. Other car clubs are more high-tech, with internet booking, but the old-fashioned pencil and calendar version works well here.

"There's a protocol—you don't book a car out for long periods without consulting other members and you only book it out for the time that's necessary, but you do strive to get it back for the time that you said you'd

get it back. Otherwise, it's first come, first served. To use the car, you collect the key, and you write the mileage as you go out and when you get
back in a log book that's kept in the glove compartment. So there's a
record of miles travelled, and that's charged at 30 pence a mile. If you pay
anything on behalf of the car club, particularly fuel, but it might be other
things like an MOT bill, that's recorded in the same log book. Then every
month, we work out how much everyone owes."

The Machynlleth car club began with a small group of friends sharing
one car. It now has 25 members sharing three cars. One of the advantages
of a car club is that members have a choice of vehicles to suit different
occasions. Andy explained to me: "We've now got quite a reasonable
range of size of cars . . . the run-around in town, the medium-sized saloon
which is reasonable for work, and then the larger estate." Recently, the
group has decided to pay a part-time administrator to keep the books up-
to-date and deal with billing, insurance renewals and the like. Nevertheless, quite a lot of tasks are still dealt with by members, such as taking
vehicles in for their MOTs.

Andy describes the informally run Machynlleth car club as "just a
bunch of mates". It is in sharp contrast to the professionally run and
high-tech car clubs that are being established in some cities. One of the
biggest of these is in Edinburgh. It has a fleet of thirty cars, shared by
hundreds of people. Members book a car on-line or by phoning a call
centre. Each member has a personal smart card. To use a car, you touch
the smart card against a detector in the windscreen. The detector checks
that you are the person who has booked the car for that particular time
slot, and the car doors unlock automatically. You get into the driving
seat, tap your pin number into the in-car computer system, take the igni-
tion key from the glove compartment, and drive off. There is no need to
write down vehicle mileages in a log book, as these are automatically
recorded by the in-car computer. The computer can also be used to make
or extend bookings. When you have finished with a car, you return it to
its dedicated car club parking bay.

Similar high-tech car clubs have been set up in Bristol, London,
Brighton and Leeds, run by people who tend to see themselves as social
entrepreneurs. After a slow start in the 1990s, the idea of the car club has
begun to catch on in Britain. For people who live where a high-tech car
club is already operating, it offers an excellent way to have occasional use
of a car without incurring the large up-front cost of buying one. But the

A car club member waves her smart card against the windscreen reader
to unlock the car. [From a photograph supplied by CarPlus]

advantage of informal schemes like the one in Machynlleth is that they can
be set up anywhere, starting with one car and maybe only four or five
friends, and growing up to three or four cars and twenty or thirty people.

Whether informal or high-tech, car clubs are an effective route to more
discriminating car use. Andy described how he uses the car club: "Well,
there's work use and that varies a bit depending on what's going on. At
the moment I use it maybe once a week for work, some weeks not at all.
And then personal use—I use it for journeys with the children, again that's
probably only once, maybe twice a week. And then once a week I might
drive across to a friend if there's no bus." Most of the time, Andy cycles,
walks or travels by bus or train. From the log book and mileage records,
it is clear that car mileages per member are universally low. Even the heav-
iest users drive less than 100 miles per week, which is about half the average for someone who drives their own car.

Andy owned a car in the past. He joined the car club because it was
convenient, but once he was a member he started to feel more strongly
about the environmental arguments for cutting car use: "It's a bit difficult

for me to disentangle my motivations. But since I've been in the car club, my motivations towards finding alternatives to car use have probably strengthened for environmental reasons, to do with climate change, primarily. The car club does provide a handy financial mechanism to encourage that, because it is relatively expensive per journey. So being part of the car club has affected my choice of public transport versus cars. I'm sure there would have been occasions in the past when I'd have travelled by car, when I had one of my own, and I'd already paid off fixed costs and it was just the cost of the fuel. And I do now think quite carefully before making those choices."

Despite what he saw as the relatively high cost of the car club per journey, Andy was still confident that membership saved him money. "It's less expensive in the car club, because the insurance and the tax are shared and the repair bills are shared. I'm sometimes shocked when you read these AA surveys on how much it actually costs to keep a car on the road. It's 40, 50 pence per mile, they say. If I had my own car it wouldn't cost me that much, I'm sure, but I think it would probably be more than 30 pence. Because I wouldn't be using it all that much, there'd be big overheads. It would be sitting there costing a lot every day when I wasn't using it."

* * *

These stories show it is possible to live a good life without being heavily dependent on cars. Karen, Teresa and Andy all had ethical reasons for wanting to limit their car use. They saw the social benefits of less car-dependent lifestyles, and the environmental advantages. But they also felt that their low-car lifestyles were personally attractive. Karen had more high-quality time with her little boy. Teresa enjoyed feeling fit and healthy because she cycled regularly, and appreciated that not running a car enabled her to work part-time. Andy liked the convenience of belonging to a car club.

But perhaps these three are oddball exceptions? Maybe they represent the peculiar 1 per cent of the population that is not particularly attached to the car? Surely there is not much point in encouraging people who fall into this tiny category to cut their own car use, when 99 per cent of people are psychologically welded to their car, and never going to change?

Andy clearly felt that this was an issue. He put it like this: "I regard the car as a means of transport. Apparently for other people it's far more than that, to do with status and personal space and fashion. It seems some part of lifestyle that they attach values to. And there's the flexibility . . . You know you've got control of it and you can make last-minute decisions. That concerns me from the point of view of expanding the car club greatly, wondering if I'm a freak in some way and it's not a viable model. Perhaps the vast majority are so attached to their cars that, however attractive the alternative is, they're just not going to budge."

This sort of concern is often expressed, but I think it is overstated. Clearly, some people have a strong emotional attachment to their car, seeing it as an extension of their personality. Equally, other people lack this attachment, and use a car in the same way that they would use any other piece of machinery. If it gets the job done by getting them from A to B, it is good enough. These people may depend on their car, but they do not love it, and they are not defined by it. There are lots of reasons why we have become so car-dependent: weak planning laws which have allowed car-oriented development and undermined local shopping; under-investment in public transport; the priority given to cars in road design, which makes walking and cycling unappealing; the large budgets dedicated to car advertising. These things combined together have made car travel into the social norm. Everything points us towards driving as the normal and easy way to travel, and it takes conscious determination to travel in any other way.

But there is nothing fixed about this. Social norms can and do change, and people's values and attitudes change with them. Drink-driving is an example of this. In 1979, the majority of adults believed that drinking and driving was not only acceptable, but necessary to a normal life. One survey found that 60 per cent of people agreed that "It's difficult to avoid some drinking and driving if you are going to have any kind of social life." But over the following twenty years, people's attitudes gradually shifted, so that by 1997 only 19 per cent of people agreed with that statement.[2] Drink-driving had changed from being socially acceptable to socially unacceptable. People no longer saw it as normal. The once-common offer, "Have one for the road", is now rarely heard.

A similar change in attitudes has occurred with smoking. In the 1950s, the upper deck of most double-decker buses was blue with cigarette smoke. People smoked at work, on trains, in pubs, cafés and restaurants. It was the social norm. Yet today, the overwhelming majority of people believe that there should be restrictions on smoking in public places. More than eight out of ten people believe smoking should be restricted at work, in indoor shopping centres, and in indoor areas at railway and bus stations. More than nine out of ten believe it should be restricted in restaurants, sport and leisure centres, banks and post offices. The one remaining public place where a significant proportion of people believe it is acceptable to smoke is the pub, but even there, views are changing fast. Between 1996 and 2004, the proportion of people believing smoking should be restricted in pubs rose from 48 per cent to 65 per cent.[3]

Today, it is normal and acceptable to hop in the car for a quick trip to the corner shop for a pint of milk. It is okay to drive the children to school, even if the distance is only half a mile along quiet residential roads. No one quivers an eyebrow if a colleague takes the car for a business trip in order to claim lucrative expenses. It is acceptable to drive a vast sports utility vehicle that guzzles fuel and spews harmful gases. It is fine for one fit and healthy person to drive alone hundreds of miles between cities, even if the train could have got them there as quickly and cheaply. It is normal to use your car as if there were no alternative, even when there is.

The cumulative damage caused by all this indiscriminate car use is much greater than any personal benefit it might confer. Unnecessary car use is every bit as antisocial as exposing other people to your cigarette smoke or risking the lives of others by driving when drunk.

It is also perfectly conceivable that attitudes will change. In the 1950s, the average smoker would have been aghast at the suggestion that he should not light up at work, on trains or in pubs and restaurants. In the 1960s, the typical man in the pub would have been outraged at the idea that he should not drive home. Attitudes to smoking in public places and drink-driving have changed, and so could attitudes to unnecessary car use.

At the moment, rather few people consciously keep their car use to a minimum. Most people do not think about this at all, or if they do, it is only fleetingly and has no effect on their travel decisions. But those who actively seek to minimise their car use have a crucial role to play. By showing that it is possible to have a good life without being entirely dependent on a car, they give other people the courage and inspiration to reduce their own car use. We are far more likely to be influenced by people we know and trust than by politicians or the media. In fact, research into the nature of influence suggests that the real opinion leaders are not the people we see on television, but our friends, family and acquaintances, and especially people within our social networks who we see as knowledgeable about a particular issue.[4] The most powerful influencers of our behaviour are the people we know. Karen, Teresa and Andy—and, perhaps, you—are the opinion leaders whose deliberate efforts to use cars responsibly could help transform public attitudes towards unnecessary car use.

Chapter 10

What does the future hold?

Dating from 1699, Queen Square in Bristol was probably the first grand residential square to be built outside London. I have a copy of an old watercolour of the original square that shows tree-lined gravel paths running between lawns on which well-to-do ladies are picnicking and boys are playing with hoops. The paths meet in the centre of the square, at a statue of King William III on horseback. Queen Square was a green lung for the city, a space for its residents to relax, enjoy nature, and see and be seen. Fifty years after the square was laid out, a Bristol poet called Mr Goldwin put it like this:

> Here elms and limes in treble order run,
> To screen our walking beauties from the sun.[1]

All this was destroyed in 1936, when a dual carriageway was built from corner to corner of the square, as part of an inner ring road for the city. Buildings were knocked down and the grass square was cut in half. At the centre of the square, the dual carriageway widened and split in two. King William was ignominiously cut off from the stately lawns and gravel paths, and marooned between two roaring streams of traffic.

By 1990, 20,000 vehicles were driving through the square every day. More cars were parked around its edges. It was noisy, the air was polluted, and the square was run-down. The vestiges of green space were inaccessible. Few people used the square. Pedestrians had to walk in the road because parked vehicles overhung the narrow pavements. Many of the fine buildings surrounding the square were vacant.[2]

This sad story of officially sanctioned vandalism could be about a public space in one of any number of towns across Britain. There are hundreds of examples of traffic-induced dereliction and of once-beautiful spaces which have become ugly concrete no man's lands. Often, people forget what was there before.

But the story of Queen Square has a happy ending. The city resolved to reclaim its public spaces from domination by cars. In 1993, the dual carriageway through the square was closed. Then the money ran out, and for five years nothing happened. Finally, one year short of the square's 300th birthday, work began to dig up the tarmac and restore the square to its earlier magnificence. The original gravel pathways and lawns were reinstated. Trees were replanted at the corners of the square. The owners of the surrounding buildings all agreed to remove the messy car parking and the traditional walls and railings were put back in front of the houses.

When I first visited Queen Square with Helen Holland, one of the city's councillors responsible for these dramatic changes, it was hard to believe that there had ever been a dual carriageway. Two mothers sat on the grass with their toddlers, enjoying a picnic, and office workers strolled and cycled past on their way home. Helen pointed out the statue of King William, once again the centrepiece of the square. Set into the ground around the base of the statue there is a large stone ring, around which runs an inscription commemorating 'the return of this historic space to the citizens of Bristol'.

* * *

The solutions that we have explored in this book offer the opportunity for many more Queen Squares. With less traffic, we will be able to use land more productively and pleasurably, instead of allocating it to soulless tarmac car parks and noisy dual carriageways. We will be able to do this not just in cities, but in small towns and suburbs that have been made desolate by the huge acreage of car parks, ring roads, junctions, roundabouts and garage forecourts that have been built in the last fifty years to cater for car-dependent shopping and commuting. Professor John Whitelegg estimated that about 170 square metres of land is tarmacked, as roads and car parks, for every car in Britain.[3] In other words, every car sterilises land covering about 25 times its actual footprint. In built-up areas, I guess that perhaps a third of the land is either dedicated to cars or rendered unattractive for other uses because of its proximity to traffic.

But the creation of more Queen Squares is not just a coincidental bonus of actions to reduce our car-dependence; it is a vital ingredient to ensure the effectiveness of the soft and small-scale ideas that we have been exploring. The reason for this is simple. Suppose that some drivers begin cycling or using the bus more often, perhaps because they have been persuaded to do so by a cut-price bus pass or new cycle parking offered by their employers, or because bus services have got better, or because the local authority has built a new cycle lane. Once these people stop driving to work, there will be fewer cars on the road and therefore less congestion. As soon as this happens, other people will notice that the traffic is better, and will decide to drive. Any benefits as a result of soft and small-scale actions will be short-lived. Traffic will simply grow to fill up the space that has been created. The technical way of putting this is to say that on busy roads where traffic levels are already suppressed by congestion, soft and small-scale actions would generate what is known as 'induced' traffic.

To prevent extra traffic filling the space created by more people cycling or using the bus, the soft and small-scale actions must be accompanied by policies for positive use of the road and parking space that is freed up. Suppose that a better bus service on a particular road is expected to entice 10 per cent of car drivers out of their cars. In that case, 10 per cent of the traffic capacity of the road should be put to another use. This could be done by making the pavements wider in places where they are too narrow. Or it might make it possible to extend the 'green man' time allowed to cross the road at pedestrian crossings. Or a dingy, unsafe pedestrian subway could be replaced with a street-level zebra crossing.

The same argument applies not only at the level of an individual road, but for an entire town. If a combination of lots of soft and small-scale projects is expected to cut traffic by, say, a quarter, over a period of about a decade, the amount of space in the town dedicated to cars can be reduced by the same amount. That would make it possible to replace a quarter of the parking spaces in the town—not all at one go, but gradually over ten years. Prime town-centre land could be used for houses, shops, restaurants or green space—far more valuable uses than a car park. Streets and squares that have become clogged with traffic and parked cars could, like Queen Square in Bristol, be returned to their original glory.

So if all of the actions we have discussed were put together, just how much traffic could we get rid of, and how much space could thus be freed for better uses? Is the estimate above of a quarter over a decade a reasonable one? And is it financially feasible, or would it cost the earth?

In 2003, the Government commissioned a study to find out whether the cumulative effects of soft actions were only marginal, which was what most people had assumed up until then, or whether they might be significant. They gave a contract to a group of six researchers of whom I was one. They asked us to concentrate on ten soft types of action: school and workplace travel plans; marketing of public transport; a technique called personalised travel planning; car clubs and car sharing; advertising campaigns; and three actions that use the latest information technology—teleworking, teleconferencing and home shopping. We set out to gather information from people who had been implementing these soft actions all over the country.

It quickly became apparent that there were many examples of success. We were impressed by the activities of the people we met. Many of them had encouraging stories to tell, some of which I have retold in this book. It was also clear that most of them had produced impressive results on tiny budgets, and were being prevented from expanding their work by the lack of resources.

Once we had gathered detailed evidence, we set out to estimate what it might be possible to achieve if all of these soft actions were implemented in the same place, at the same time, and as intensively as possible within the limits of what is practically achievable. We concluded that the soft actions we had looked at could indeed potentially cut car traffic by a quarter (26 per cent) in the busiest places at the busiest times.[4] So the answer to our first question is that soft actions alone have the potential to deliver substantial cuts in car traffic. They could reduce traffic to something like school holiday levels.

However, our estimate did not assume any physical change in the transport choices available to people—no major networks of cycle lanes, no transformation of the bus service. It was based on the changes in people's travel behaviour that were already being achieved, using the less-than-perfect transport system that we currently have. If the soft actions were coupled with small-scale physical improvements to make it easier and nicer to walk, cycle or take the bus, the potential for change would be even greater. It is difficult to put a figure on this, but in Freiburg the number of car driver trips per car fell by about 20 per cent over the period that the city was building its bicycle network and improving its public transport.[5]

The next question was whether it would cost the earth. Very approximately, I estimated that the cost of enough soft actions to cut rush hour car traffic by a quarter would be about £5 per year for every citizen of a town. Another way of putting our cost estimates is that the Government would have to spend about 1.5 pence for every car kilometre that was taken off the road.

This estimate is only for soft actions, and we did not cost small-scale physical changes like cycle paths and better buses, which would be more expensive. However, even these physical changes turn out to be well within the budgets that the Government and local councils already spend on transport. In another study, I worked with a coalition of environmental groups including Transport 2000 and Friends of the Earth to estimate the cost of a comprehensive programme of small-scale measures, of the sort that have been described in this book. From that work, the cost of the types of small-scale measures we have been looking at comes to about £35 per citizen per year.[6]

If you add together the costs suggested by the two studies, the rough cost of the actions we have looked at in this book would be £40 per citizen a year. Figures like these date quickly. But what do not change are relative proportions. Our country's spending programme for transport over the decade from 2000 to 2010 is equivalent to £360 per citizen, per year. The bulk of this budget is consumed by large-scale engineering projects, including road schemes costing billions of pounds. Ultimately, the money comes from our taxes. Ironically, if just a tenth of the amount we currently spend on transport was dedicated to soft and small-scale measures, we would need to build fewer roads and the total tax bill would almost certainly be less. Soft and small-scale actions do not cost the earth, and in fact they represent incredibly good value for money.

* * *

It is possible to cease to be so dependent upon cars, and if we did this, the places where we live would be cleaner, safer, more peaceful, and healthier. They would be more like some of the places that delight us when we visit them on holiday. In cities, there would be more space for pavement cafés and shady trees. In the suburbs, children would be able to go on their bikes to visit their friends, as their parents once did. In the countryside, we would be able to find peaceful places once more. Instead of the dull roar of the dual carriageway, we could hear birdsong and rivers again. If we used cars with more discrimination, we would also be healthier, happier, less stressed and fitter. We would start to put the brakes on the climate change which is set to cause such dramatic and disturbing damage to our children's planet.

The problems caused by cars are of concern to many people. When a government survey asked what environmental trends or issues would cause most concern in twenty years' time, the most frequently raised issue was traffic, which was mentioned first by more than half of the people who were questioned.[7] There is no doubt that car-sickness lies within what a social scientist might term our 'sphere of concern', that is, the spectrum of issues that perturbs us. But at the same time we feel helpless. We feel that the problem is outside what might be called our sphere of influence.

But look at where the good ideas to cure our car-sickness are coming from: they are coming from people like you and me. Take the successful school travel work we saw in Merseyside. I know that the wacky idea of a walking bus came from Australian environmentalist David Engwicht, via a school in the south of England, and then spread to Merseyside and the rest of the UK and around the world. I also know that a woman called Katy Green who worked for a voluntary organisation in Leicester called Children Today was one of the earliest people to work with children to design safe walking routes to school, and this in turn led to traffic calming, low-speed zones and cycle lanes around hundreds, perhaps eventually thousands, of schools across Britain. Think of car clubs, like the one that Andy R. belongs to in Machynlleth or the high-tech one in Edinburgh. I think that Michael Glotz-Richter was one of the first people to set up a car club in Germany, in the town of Bremen, and I think he may have got the idea from someone in Berlin who started it all by sharing a car with his brother. I think John Adams, the university professor whom we met in Chapter Eight, had a share in bringing that idea to Britain, where Edinburgh council became interested and raised some money to back the first high-tech scheme. The home zones we heard about in Chapter Six had their origins in the 1970s in the Netherlands, but they came to Britain via a woman called Barbara Preston, who wrote about them, and who inspired me and Tim Gill, a friend who worked for the Children's Play Council, to campaign for them. The result was that other people heard about them on the radio, including a woman called Charmian Boyd who lived in an Ealing street that was too dangerous for her to let her son play in. She launched a community group to campaign for a home zone and got funding for one of the first in Britain.

These are the pieces of the story that I know. There are hundreds more people who are playing a part in these changes. There are thousands more who by their actions are showing that it is possible to lead a good life without a car, or while using a car sparingly.

Notes

Chapter 1: Cars 'R' Us

1. Ivan Illich, *Energy and Equity*, Marion Boyars, London, 1974.

2. The detailed breakdown of the calculation is as follows. For a middle-of-the-range car, driven 10,000 miles per year, the AA puts standing costs at 36 pence per mile (road tax, insurance, cost of capital, depreciation and breakdown cover) and running costs at 20 pence per mile (petrol, tyres, service labour costs, replacement parts, parking and tolls). Median annual salary is £22,060 (gross), equivalent to a net hourly wage of £11. Hence the time taken to earn the money to pay standing and running costs of the car is 510 hours. From the National Travel Survey, the average speed of car trips (allowing for time spent in traffic jams as well as time spent in motion) is 23.4 miles an hour. It will take 427 hours to clock up 10,000 miles over the course of a year. I have assumed that the average driver will spend one hour per week on average cleaning their car, taking it for repair, filling it with petrol, pumping the tyres and so on. I have further assumed that they will spend five minutes on average at the beginning of each trip looking for the car keys, walking to the car, and de-icing it in winter; and a similar time at the end of each trip finding a space to park and walking from the parking space to their destination. These small tasks add 254 hours per year. Finally, the Nationwide Building Society reports that a single garage adds 11.1 per cent to the cost of a house. For an average house costing £158,000, this is equivalent to £17,538 which, at 6 per cent interest per year, would add £1,052 to annual mortgage repayments, requiring another 96 hours of work at average net pay of £11 per hour.

3. Bob Ogley, *Kent: A Chronicle of the Century*, Volume 3, 1950-1974, Froglets Publications, Kent, 1998.

Chapter 2: Cars—the ultimate mixed blessing

1. For the Department for the Environment, Transport and the Regions, 'The Impact of Large Foodstores on Market Towns and District Centres', C. B. Hillier Parker and Savell Bird & Axon, The Stationery Office, London, 1998.

2. *Ghost town Britain: the threat from economic globalisation to livelihoods, liberty and local economic freedom*, New Economics Foundation, 2002.

3. Hillier Parker and Savell Bird & Axon, *op. cit.*

4. 'Rural transport futures: transport solutions for a thriving countryside', Transport 2000 Trust, the Countryside Agency and Citizens Advice, 2003.

5. Article by Margaret Effenberg in *Transport Retort 23/3*, Summer 2000, Transport 2000.

6. John Adams 'The social implications of hypermobility' in *Project on Environmentally Sustainable Transport (EST). The economic and social implications of sustainable transportation. Proceedings from the Ottawa workshop*, Organisation for Economic Co-operation and Development, Paris, 1999.

7. Robert D. Putnam, *Bowling Alone: The collapse and revival of American community*, Simon & Schuster, New York, 2000.

8. 'At least five a week. Evidence on the impact of physical activity and its relationship to health. A report from the Chief Medical Officer', Department of Health, London, 2004.

9. Report on Mintel poll, BBC News, 4 February 2004.

10. *Healthy Lifestyles: Healthy Halos, Healthy Aware or Reckless Risk-takers*, Mintel, 2001.

11. Andrew M. Prentice and Susan A. Jebb, 'Obesity in Britain: gluttony or sloth?' in *British Medical Journal*, Volume 311, 1995, pp.437–439.

12. These studies are referenced in a report by Nick Cavill and Adrian Davis, 'Cycling and health: a briefing for the Regional Cycling Development Team', AEA Technology / National Cycling Strategy Board, 2003.

13. A. Colin Bell, Keyou Ge and Barry M. Popkin, 'The road to obesity or the path to prevention: motorised transportation and obesity in China', *Obesity Research*, Volume 10, number 4, 2002, pp.277–283.

14. The official figures reported by the Department for Transport indicate that on average nine people are killed on British roads each day; 85 are seriously injured; and 675 are slightly injured. However, these figures, based on crashes which are reported to the police, are known to be underestimates. By comparing police data with hospital admissions, the Department for Transport estimates that the actual number of serious injuries is about 2.8 times the reported police figure, and that the actual number of slight injuries is about 1.7 times the police figure. Of course, hospital data probably under-record the number of slight injuries, so even using this adjustment we may be under-counting the real extent of injury. Data on damage-only crashes, where nobody is injured, are even more difficult to obtain, but the Department for Transport and the Scottish Executive variously estimate the number of damage-only crashes as between seven and eighteen times higher than the number of crashes where a person is injured.

15. 'Britain actually "in love with speed cameras", new survey shows', Transport 2000 press release, 14 February 2004.

16. Ros Coward, 'Phoney populism: don't pander to the ordinary bloke's addiction to cars', *The Guardian*, 25 November 2004.

17. *Digest of UK Energy Statistics 2004*, Table 1.1.5, 'Energy Consumption by Final User'.

18. Royal Commission on Environmental Pollution, 'Energy—the changing climate', Twenty-second report, Cm 4749, 2000.

19. Chris D. Thomas, Alison Cameron, Rhys E. Green and sixteen others, 'Extinction Risk from Climate Change', *Nature*, volume 427, 8 January 2004, pp.144–148.

20. Royal Commission on Environmental Pollution, *op. cit.*

21. Foresight Flood and Coastal Defence Project, 'Future Flooding Executive Summary', Office of Science and Technology, 2004.

22. *Ibid.*

23. 'Climate Change 2001: Synthesis Report. Summary for policymakers', Intergovernmental Panel on Climate Change, 2001.

24 P. M. Cox, R. A. Betts, M. Collins, P. Harris, C. Huntingford, C. D. Jones, 'Amazon dieback under climate-carbon cycle projections for the 21st century', Hadley Centre technical note 42, Meteorological Office, 2003.

25. 'Amazon under threat', Greenpeace International briefing, 2004.

26. 'Climate warning as Siberia melts', *New Scientist*, 11 August 2005.

27. *Contraction and Convergence*, Global Commons Institute, Schumacher Briefing No. 5, undated.

28. Mayer Hillman with Tina Fawcett, *How We Can Save the Planet*, Penguin Books, 2004.

29. Steve Purnell, Jillian Beardwood and John Elliott, 'The Effects of Strategic Network Changes on Traffic' in *World Transport Policy and Practice* 5(2), 1999, pp.28–48.

30. Report of public local inquiry into objections, Volume 1: main report, M74 special road (Fullarton Road to west of Kingston Bridge) orders, 2004.

31. 'M74 Link Gets Go Ahead', Scottish Executive news release, 24 March 2005

Chapter 3: Soft, small, stubborn: principles of de-motorisation

1. Werner Brög, Erhard Erl and Helen Grey-Smith, 'The Perth experience: reducing the use of cars—the homeopathic way', Paper presented to seminar of the Greater London Assembly, 'Reducing traffic congestion in London: policy options other than road pricing', 2002.

2. Socialdata, 'Darlington: Sustainable travel demonstration town travel behaviour research baseline survey 2004', report for Darlington Borough Council, 2005.

3. Werner Brög, personal communication with the author

4. Lynn Sloman and Nat Taplin, Transport for Quality of Life, 'Getting About the Dyfi Valley: An assessment of local people's priorities for transport', Communities First Bro Ddyfi, Camad, Ecodyfi and Powys County Council, 2004.

5. Socialdata, 'Switching to Public Transport', International Union of Public Transport, undated.

6. Jillian Anable, ' "Complacent car addicts" or "aspiring environmentalists"? Identifying travel behaviour segments using attitude theory', *Transport Policy* Volume 12 issue 1, 2005, pp.65–78.

Chapter 4: Soft solutions to de-motorise the rush hour

1. Carey Newson, Sally Cairns and Adrian Davis, 'Making school travel plans work: experience from English case studies', Report commissioned by Department for Transport, from Transport 2000 Trust, University College London, Adrian Davis Associates, Sustrans, Cleary Hughes Associates and Transport for Quality of Life, forthcoming.

2. 'Assessment of Attitudes to, and Potential Take-up of, Additional Home to School Transport', Department for Transport, 2002.

3. 'Why high quality cyclist training is essential for cycling promotion and how it can be delivered', City of York Council, unpublished paper, 2001.

4. Roger Mackett, 'Making children's lives more active', Centre for Transport Studies, University College London, updated edition, 2004.

5. Sally Cairns, Adrian Davis, Carey Newson and Camilla Swiderska, 'Making travel plans work: Case study summaries', Report commissioned by Department for Transport, from Transport 2000 Trust, University College London and Adrian Davis Associates, 2002.

6. Donald C. Shoup, 'Evaluating the effects of cashing out employer-paid parking: eight case studies', *Transport Policy* Volume 4, issue 4, 1997, pp.201–216.

7. Jillian Anable, Alistair Kirkbride, Lynn Sloman, Carey Newson, Sally Cairns and Phil Goodwin, 'Smarter Choices: changing the way we travel, case study reports', Report commissioned by the Department for Transport, from University College London, Transport for Quality of Life, Robert Gordon University and Eco-Logica, 2004.

8. Peter Hopkinson and Peter James, 'The BT Options 2000: a pilot study of its environmental and social impacts', 2001.

9. P. Hopkinson, P. James and T. Maruyama, 'Teleworking at BT: the economic, environmental and social impacts of its Workabout scheme', Report as part of the SUSTEL programme, 2002.

10. Peter Hopkinson and Peter James, 'UK report on national SUSTEL fieldwork', 2003.

11. Sally Cairns, Lynn Sloman, Carey Newson, Jillian Anable, Alistair Kirkbride, and Phil Goodwin, 'Smarter Choices: changing the way we travel, final report', Commissioned by the Department for Transport, from University College London, Transport for Quality of Life, Robert Gordon University and Eco-Logica, 2004.

Chapter 5: Better public transport, or why buses run around empty

1. Transport 2000 Trust, the Countryside Agency and Citizens Advice, 'Rural transport futures: transport solutions for a thriving countryside', 2003.

2. More details of the Aylesbury, Bristol and Perth bus marketing campaigns are in Cairns *et al.*, *Smarter Choices, op. cit.*

3. 'One' train company news release, 'Bittern line continues to boom—passenger journeys up', 13 June 2005.

4. More details of the improvements in bus services in Brighton are in Cairns et al., *Smarter Choices, op. cit.*

5. 'The case for investing in London's buses: presenting the results of the London Buses strategic review', Transport for London, 2003.

6. *Rural transport futures, op. cit.*

Chapter 6: Cycling without Spandex

1. Ton Welleman, 'Dutch experience with government transport policy', Paper to Velomondiale Conference, 2000.

2. Ton Welleman, 'The autumn of the Bicycle Master Plan: after the plans, the products', undated, http://www.communitybike.org/cache/autumn_bike_master_plan.html

3. Heath Maddox, 'Another look at Germany's bicycle boom: implications for local transportation policy and planning strategy in the USA', in *World Transport Policy and Practice*, Volume 7, number 3, 2001, pp.44–48.

4. Felix FitzRoy and Ian Smith, 'Public transport demand in Freiburg: why did patronage double in a decade?', *Transport Policy*, Volume 5, 1998, pp.163–173.

5. *Ibid.*

6. John Parkin, 'Comparison of cycle proportions for the journey to work from the 1981, 1991 and 2001 censuses', *Traffic Engineering and Control*, Volume 44(8), September 2003, pp.299–302.

7. Accent Marketing and Research, 'The near market for cycling in London', Transport for London, 2004.

8. Office for National Statistics Omnibus Survey January 2001, reported in *Attitudes to local transport issues*, Department for Transport, undated.

9. Anker Lohmann-Hansen and Harry Lahrmann, *The BikeBus'ter project in Aarhus*, Traffic Research Group, Aalborg University, undated. The Aarhus work is also reviewed in *Smarter Choices (op. cit.*, p.184). The original name for the project was BikeBus'ter (with the inverted comma emphasising that the project was intended to stimulate bus travel as well as cycling), but an inverted comma in the middle of a word is so distracting that I have not used it.

Chapter 7: Grand design: the space between buildings

1. Cesare Marchetti, 'Anthropological invariants in travel behavior', *Technological Forecasting and Social Change*, Volume 47, 1994, pp.75–88.

2. Peter W. G. Newman and Jeffrey R. Kenworthy, 'The land use–transport connection: An overview', *Land Use Policy*, Volume 13, number 1, 1996, pp.1–22.

3. Cesare Marchetti, *op. cit.*

4. Jeffrey Kenworthy and Felix Laube, 'Patterns of automobile dependence in cities: an international overview of key physical and economic dimensions with some implications for urban policy', *Transportation Research* Part A Volume 33, pp.691–723, 1999.

5. I. Cameron, T. J. Lyons and J. R. Kenworthy, 'Trends in vehicle kilometres of travel in world cities, 1960-1990: underlying drivers and policy responses', *Transport Policy*, Volume 11, 2004, pp.287–298.

6. 'Driven to spend', Surface Transportation Policy Project, 2000.

7. Jeffrey Kenworthy and Felix Laube, *op. cit.*

8. 'Community Attitude Survey', City of Phoenix, July 2004.

9. Jan Gehl, 'The challenge of making a human quality in the city', paper to City Challenge conference, Perth, 1992, quoted in Peter Newman and Jeffrey Kenworthy *op. cit.*

10. Jan Gehl and Lars Gemzøe, *New City Spaces*, The Danish Architectural Press, 2001.

11. *Ibid.*

12. David Engwicht, *Towards an Eco-city: Calming the traffic,* Envirobook, Sydney, 1992.

13. Robert Cervero and Carolyn Radisch, 'Travel choices in pedestrian versus automobile oriented neighborhoods', *Transport Policy*, Volume 3, number 3, 1996, pp.127–141.

14. Carey Curtis, 'Can strategic planning contribute to a reduction in car-based travel?' *Transport Policy*, Volume 3, number 1/2, 1996, pp.55–65.

15. Patrick Lingwood, Memorandum (WTC28) to 'Walking in Towns and Cities', the Eleventh Report by the House of Commons Select Committee on Environment, Transport and Regional Affairs, HC 167–II, 2001.

Chapter 8: Why the political system cannot tackle transport

1. 'Attitudes to Congestion on Motorways and Other Roads', Department for Transport, 2005.

2. *Ibid.*, and 'Attitudes to Road Pricing', Department for Transport, 2004.

3. 'Attitudes to roads, congestion and congestion charging', Department for Transport, 2004.

4. Simon Jenkins, 'What is the point of Mr Darling?', *Evening Standard*, London, 12 May 2005.

5. 'Vehicle speeds in Great Britain 2003', Department for Transport, 2004.

6. Socialdata, 'Darlington: Sustainable travel demonstration town travel behaviour research baseline survey 2004', report for Darlington Borough Council, 2005.

7. 'Report of the OECD policy meeting on sustainable consumption and individual travel behaviour', Organisation for Economic Co-operation and Development, Paris, 9-10 January 1997.

8. John Adams, 'Transport choices', Article in *Transport Retort*, the magazine of Transport 2000, volume 17/1, January / February 1994.

9. Standing Advisory Committee on Trunk Road Assessment, 'Transport and the Economy', report to Department for Environment, Transport and the Regions, 1999.

10. 'Monitoring the effects. EMITS (Environmental Monitoring of Integrated Transport Strategies)', Oxfordshire County Council, 2000.

11. 'Living Streets: a guide to cutting traffic and reclaiming street space', Transport 2000 Trust, 1999.

12. Accent Marketing and Research, 'Town Centres Survey 2003-4', Report for Transport for London, 2004.

13. My calculation, based on figures for average spend per visit, frequency of visit and travel mode split for local suburban town centres, from *ibid*.

Chapter 9: Learning not to drive

1. David Engwicht, *op. cit*, p.187.

2. Nick Cavill, personal communication with the author.

3. Deborah Lader and Eileen Goddard, 'Smoking-related behaviour and attitudes', Office for National Statistics, 2004.

4. 'The New Persuaders: the changing nature of influence', Opinion Leader Research, London, 2003.

Chapter 10: What does the future hold?

1. Pat Hughes, Jane Root and Christopher Heath, 'The History and Development of Queen Square', for Bristol City Council, 1996. Mr Goldwin's poem was written in 1751.

2. I am grateful to Chris Heath of Bristol City Council for telling me the story of Queen Square.

3. John Whitelegg, *Transport and land take*, CPRE, 1994.

4. Cairns *et al.*, *Smarter Choices, op. cit.* Our calculations suggested that if the ten soft actions were implemented together, they could potentially cut the amount of car traffic in the urban rush hour by 26 per cent. Total traffic (including lorries and vans as well as cars) would fall by 21 per cent.

5. This calculation is complex because, in the real world, many things change at the same time. Over the period that Freiburg was building its cycle network and improving public transport, its population grew, and the proportion of people owning cars also grew, the latter probably because of a general increase in incomes and decrease in the cost of buying and running a car. The best we can do is to normalise the figures, or try to take these variables out of the equation. In 1982, Freiburg had a population of 201,000, there were 65,509 cars, and 29

per cent of each Freiburg resident's trips were made as a car driver. By 1995 the population had risen to 227,000 and there were 82,830 cars and at about the same time (the figure is actually for the year 1999), 26 per cent of trips were as a car driver. If we assume that the total number of trips per person did not change, which is a reasonable assumption, we can calculate what happened to the number of car driver trips per car. The arithmetic is:

Change in car driver trips per car =

$$\frac{[(0.26T \times 227,000)/82,830 - (0.29T \times 201,000)/65,509]}{(0.29T \times 201,000)/65,509}$$

In this equation, T is the total number of trips each Freiburg resident makes per day. This gives a reduction in car driver trips of 20 per cent.

6. Way to Go coalition of 25 environment, transport and social justice organisations 'Paying for better transport: costing the Way to Go manifesto', Transport 2000 and Friends of the Earth, 2004. This document gave an annual cost of £1.7 billion (capital plus revenue) for a comprehensive programme of small-scale measures in England only.

7. 'Survey of public attitudes to quality of life and to the environment—2001', Department for Environment, Food and Rural Affairs, 2002.

Index